3 Queneau: Zazie dans le métro

Critical Guides to French Texts

EDITED BY ROGER LITTLE, WOLFGANG VAN EMDEN, DAVID WILLIAMS

QUENEAU

Zazie dans le métro

W. D. Redfern

Reader at the Department of French Studies
University of Reading

Grant & Cutler Ltd
1980

© Grant & Cutler Ltd
  1980
ISBN 0 7293 0086 2

I.S.B.N. 84-499-4366-3

DEPÓSITO LEGAL: v. 150 - 1981

Printed in Spain by
Artes Gráficas Soler, S.A., Valencia
for
GRANT & CUTLER LTD
11 BUCKINGHAM STREET, LONDON, W.C.2.

Contents

For Sam

'Car pourquoi ne demanderait-on pas un certain effort du lecteur?'

QUENEAU

1 *Queneau: Life*

Raymond Queneau was a man of many parts, some of them congenitally private.[1] He once said, in an interview with Georges Charbonnier, that his favourite character in fiction was Rabelais's Trouillogan, who always gave only evasive answers to questions (p. 12). Queneau went on to say that, as soon as he uttered an opinion, he saw at once that he could equally well have said something diametrically opposed, a possibility which occurs also to Zazie herself: 'Pourquoi qu'on dit des choses et pas d'autres?' (p. 87). But, as Diderot, another splendid humorist and encyclopaedic intelligence, proposed for the reading by others of his own paradoxical nature: let the contradictions, doubts and divergences take care of themselves, and concentrate on the periodic points of return, the constants. In this way, we may at least approximate to Queneau. In other ways, too, perhaps. By trying, for instance, to match his idiosyncratic tone, and by simulating a comparably anarchic respect for order: back-references, criss-crosses, and inversions.

Queneau was born in 1903, in Le Havre (Normandy). His parents ran a prosperous draper's shop. He seems not to have been particularly happy at school, where he spent much of his time writing parodies, poems and adventure-stories. He first acquired what was to be his lifelong familiarity and obsession with spoken French, in all its multiple varieties, from popular literature, and then, in the flesh, during his military service in North Africa. Armies, whatever else they are, constitute great linguistic melting-pots. Even as a child, he developed encyclopaedic interests ('Si l'on s'écrie "livresque", je n'y contredirai pas', he admitted in *Bâtons, chiffres et lettres* (p. 11)). While still a boy, he read from cover to cover the first fat volume of the Larousse Dictionary, a feat he compared in *Bords* with that of the Autodidact in Sartre's *La Nausée*, working

---

[1] Page numbers in brackets refer to the work by Queneau specified, and, in the main body of the study, to the Gallimard ("Folio") edition of *Zazie dans le métro*. References in the style (*18*, p. 43) refer to the numbered critical texts on Queneau in the Bibliography.

his way, in alphabetical order, through the collections of the same municipal library in Le Havre, (pp. 120-21). To this panoramic opening, Queneau gradually added more specific interests in foreign literatures, the history of religions, mathematics, linguistics and philosophy, especially the Greeks and the leading nineteenth-century German philosopher, Hegel, on whom he edited an important study. The eminent biologist Jean Rostand found no errors in Queneau's scientific knowledge as displayed in his poem *Petite cosmogonie portative* (*28*, p. 491). And Queneau's mathematics were of a quality to bring him invitations to address professionals and to write in their journals. Apart from these central and obviously important areas, he was also fascinated by more marginal subjects. For example, he spent some years at the Bibliothèque Nationale compiling dossiers on nineteenth-century 'fous littéraires' (literary, but also scientific, cranks). He wrote later, in *Bâtons, chiffres et lettres*, that most of them were 'des paranoïaques réactionnaires et des bavards gâteux' (p. 261). But he intercalated chunks of this otherwise unpublishable research material into his novel *Les Enfants du limon*, where he defined madness as 'l'auto-déification d'un individu dans lequel ne se reconnaît aucun collectif' (p. 294).

Queneau travelled abroad a fair amount (e.g. to Greece and later to the United States), but he was always most at home exploring, on foot or by bus, the nooks and crannies of his adopted stamping-ground, Paris. (There is plenty of evidence of this familiarity, admittedly subverted in burlesque fashion, in *Zazie dans le métro*.) I once heard the Professor of French History at Oxford, Richard Cobb, in the course of a lecture, recite lyrically all the bus routes and numbers in Paris, as they figure in the novels of Queneau. In this way, as in his eye for social behaviour, Queneau acts as a remembrancer for an often vanishing reality. At one stage he hawked paper-napkins around cheapjack Paris restaurants, where he gained that acquaintance with the seamier side of French cuisine, so marvellously evoked in *Zazie dans le métro*. For some time in the 1930s, he ran too a column called 'Connaissez-vous Paris?' in the daily paper, *L'Intransigeant*. The countryside he often had his doubts about. A character in *Saint-Glinglin* speaks of 'le solennel emmerdement de la ruralité' (p. 129). On the other hand, even of towns a Queneau hero, in *Les Derniers Jours*, can maintain: 'Il n'aimait pas la ville, mais sa topographie. Il ne connaissait que le squelette et non la chair' (p. 113). Death walks the streets of Queneau's far from invariably comic universe, as Veuve Mouaque in *Zazie dans le métro* finds to her ultimate cost. Shakespeare's Yorick turns up in disguise in several of Queneau's novels (e.g. *Un Rude Hiver*, *Les Derniers Jours*).

In the 1920s, Queneau mixed for a short time in Surrealist groups, but soon left after a personal disagreement with the Surrealist 'Pope', André Breton. This episode furnished the material for Queneau's least convincing book, a *roman à clef*, *Odile*. He was also, briefly, a member of Boris Souvarine's 'Cercle Communiste Démocratique', a loose grouping composed of a motley collection of excluded Communists and ex-Surrealists. Like the hero of *Odile*, Queneau was always nearer to Plato than to Marx, more drawn to the eternal problems of Being than to the time-bound issues of political and economic existence. From his early thirties up to his death in 1976, Queneau earned his living mainly by working for the leading French publishers, Gallimard, as a literary editor, occasional translator from English, and eventually director in charge of the large-scale 'Encyclopédie de la Pléiade', which taught him, he claimed modestly in *Bords*, how little he knew (p. 27). Though never a convinced joiner of groups, he belonged from the 1950s until his death to the 'Collège de 'Pataphysique', an institution of serious looniness which has counted amongst its regulars the Absurdist playwright Ionesco, several mathematicians, writers and literary critics. 'Pataphysics, whose spiritual ancestor and prime mover was the anarchic, pre-Surrealist, turn-of-the-century writer, Alfred Jarry, has been defined as 'the science of imaginary solutions'. All its devotees subscribe to the belief that, philosophically speaking, all things and all values are equal, that contraries do not exist, and that only particulars are of interest. I am reminded of the only entirely valid generalisation ever uttered, by an American professor, who said, incontrovertibly: 'The world is divided up between people who believe that you can say "The world is divided up . . .", and those who do not'.

'To infancy, o Lord, again I come That I my manhood may improve.' This epigraph from Thomas Traherne to Queneau's autobiographical verse-novel, *Chêne et chien*, reminds us that, for some years in the 1930s, Queneau underwent psycho-analytic treatment. From a few clues scattered through his works (especially *Saint-Glinglin*), it seems likely that he suffered from the not uncommon urge to liquidate his father (who had nourished pro-German sentiments in the First World War), and to return to the maternal breast. There is no means for an outsider of knowing how effective the treatment was, but the literary exploitation of these anxieties in *Un Rude Hiver* produced, in a typical twist, a very likeable reactionary hero caught up in a tender and despairing love-story. Queneau also suffered a good deal from asthma during his youth and early manhood. The poet, des Cigales, in *Loin de Rueil*, is afflicted by a disease called *ontalgie*: the pain of being, an existential sickness. It resembles asthma, but is, a friend claims, 'posher'. This wry joke about a serious and often excruciating disability—a young man in *Les Enfants du limon*, similarly afflicted, declares pain to be an absolute (p. 205)—reminds us not to take Queneau too heavily, nor too lightly. We should take him, as he takes us, as he is.

2 Queneau: Comedy, language and philosophy

I cannot offer a comprehensive theory of Queneau's comic art, largely because Queneau himself, despite his interest in mathematical games and formal structures, was the most anti-systematic of men. *Les Enfants du limon* contains an 'Encyclopédie des Sciences Inexactes', and one of Queneau's favourite books was Flaubert's *Bouvard et Pécuchet*, a whole-hearted onslaught against *l'esprit de système*. The only generalisation about comedy which has ever convinced me is that laughter is one of only three phenomena which occupy our *total* attention: the other two are the sneeze and the orgasm. Even so, I had better run helter-skelter through some of the major theories of comedy over the centuries, if only to put Queneau into perspective, and bearing always in mind what a philosopher once said: that the funniest thing about comedy is the theories people cook up to explain it.

For Plato, laughter was essentially provoked either by malice or by envy. For Aristotle, it was sparked off by any ludicrous spectacle, especially, and here Cicero chimes in with him, any physical or moral deformity. Such theories obviously harbour a strong dose of aggressiveness, and the English seventeenth-century thinker, Thomas Hobbes, believed that comedy depended on a sense of superiority over the person being mocked. Molière, representing a different tradition, took a perhaps more helpful attitude, in that he thought laughter might assist in the correcting of other people's vices or errors. In the early twentieth century, the French thinker, Bergson, placed all the stress, in his theory of comedy, on the mechanisation of human attributes. In other words, whenever we behave in a way that resembles a machine or a physical object, we become automatically laughable. Freud tried to explain comedy as a 'device of psychic economy': that is, in being amused, we evacuate or displace tensions which might otherwise be too difficult for us to cope with. Now, all these theories seem to me to place the emphasis on laughing against others, and to undervalue the importance of laughing with them. They concentrate, in short, on the violent aspects of comedy (which are undeniably basic to it), and overlook its gentler and more sociable functions.

It is of course possible to have comedy without words. We have only to think of silent films, or mime. But, for a writer, it is language itself that is the main source of the comic. The funny noises we make, the daft ideas we try to express, the weird verbal structures we concoct, these are Queneau's basic material, his subject-matter. As a writer, Queneau was always obsessed with the differences between written and spoken French. (He openly admitted, in *Bâtons, chiffres et lettres*, that other contemporary writers, like Céline and Prévert, had had comparable aims of demo-cratising literary French, and that he himself made no claims to linguistic originality (p. 14)). It was his trip to Greece in the early 1930s that first alerted him to that kind of gap between the two languages. He already knew classical Greek from his readings, but in Greece he heard the spoken, demotic variety, which both echoes and strongly diverges from the literary version. About the same time, he was also much taken by the way that James Joyce, in *Ulysses*, handled the vernacular, and by Joyce's readiness to switch styles, from the most lofty to the most down-to-earth, within a chapter, or even within a sentence. Similarly, Queneau was struck by Joyce's masterful reworking of the Homer poem in a modern context. Queneau had for some time been increasingly aware that the written French language had become what has been called 'an Esperanto for intellectuals'. He pointed, like several others before him, to the eighteenth-century as the key age of the French tongue's triumph as a universal, diplomatic mode of discourse. He was not alone in thinking that the great nineteenth-century French grammarians like Littré had in effect refrigerated the French language in order to make it keep longer. As a result, literary French had become, if not a dead, then at least a freeze-wrapped, language. For example, some of its cherished forms (the past historic, or the imperfect subjunctive) have all but vanished from spoken French. The reaction of some linguistic conservatives, and indeed linguistic racialists— for Queneau pointed out in *Bâtons, chiffres et lettres* (p. 92) that many in this respect too were eager to preserve the purity of the national stock—to this widening chasm, and to the growing pheno-menon called *franglais* (i.e. the taking over wholesale into French of English or American words), has been to send up S.O.S. signals and to bewail the imminent death of French as a separate and unique language. Queneau's response was different. He felt that, as language is a matter of convention, and as we should do in Rome as the Romans do, then the borrowing of foreign words is no crime. No linguistic protectionist, he saw *franglais* as a potential source of new riches rather than as an impoverishment. It fitted in, besides, with his own taste for slang, coinages, portmanteau words, and so on.

Queneau had taken over from the work, *Le Langage*, by the French linguistician Vendryès the notion that the syntax of spoken French is in many ways closer to that of a Red Indian language like Chinook, than it is to the beautifully ordered cadences of an André Gide. The syntax of spoken French is much more broken up and redistributed than in the literary variety. Thus juxtaposition supersedes subordination, and emotional emphasis rather than logic dictates the sequence of words. Queneau, in *Bâtons, chiffres et lettres* offers a telling example of this occurrence: 'On n'entendra jamais dire: "N'est-ce point Bobet qui, l'année dernière, avait déjà gagné le Tour de France?" mais plutôt: "Il l'avait déjà gagné le Tour de France l'année dernière Bobet?" ' (p. 80). In addition to syntax, there is the spelling question. Queneau was convinced, with every right, that current spelling orthodoxy is also a matter of pure convention, and is often, indeed, based on false etymologies. It would be more honest if we spelt as we spoke: phonetically. But this of course is a pipe-dream, and even, as Queneau recognised in *Voyage en Grèce*, probably a non-problem (p. 226). These different perceptions about language encouraged Queneau for many years to promote the idea that a new language was needed for literature: *le néo-français*. Even in *Zazie dans le métro*, however, this *néo-français* is used parsimoniously, and a few years before his death, in *Voyage en Grèce*, Queneau admitted that the desired language revolution, the radicalisation of literary French, had not in fact come about, nor was it ever likely to. 'Le français normal,' he concluded, 'poursuit son cours' (p. 222). Furthermore, we should stress that Queneau always envisaged the coexistence of the established and the innovatory languages. Linguistically, Queneau is no extremist, but a fellow-traveller. The force of his original argument yet holds good. If human beings insist on growing up, why not language too? He urged, in effect: take the corsets off the written language; Words Liberation!

It often seems that his novels are meant to be spoken, read aloud, rather than silently perused. For his games with the form of words and with the restructuring of sentences produce a situation where what was already familiar from daily practice to the ear is forcibly made familiar to the eye. He helps thereby to complete our linguistic education by pulling together the separate strands of our various responses to language. In this refusal to support traditional hierarchies of value (i.e. the written seen as superior to the spoken), he is acting as a truly democratic writer. Perhaps surprisingly, his best-selling book before *Zazie* (and it was even set to music and performed on the halls by Les Frères Jacques) was *Exercices de style*. In this book, Queneau, inspired by a concert of Bach variations, performs ninety-nine permutations on a banal topic (an insignificant incident on a Paris bus). He recounts the happening in Alexandrines, in the form of a Japanese *haiku*, in code, and in a whole range of styles from the most noble to the most vulgar. In so doing, he reminds us that language is our natural habitat and our main instrument of communication; that the world we live in is, to a very large extent, made up of words.

Now, one of the things some people, or perhaps all people at some moment, do with language is to philosophise: to put ideas into words, to verbalise thought or intuitions. Any writer faces the ancient problem of how to animate, to embody, ideas; how to make concepts sing, weep, waver, strut, cringe, insist, query. In some of Queneau's weaker fiction, he falls into the old trap of intercalating blocks of speculation, but far more often he imagines dramatic situations which *show* the thought without excessive telling or other overselling. Besides, it is always Queneau's voice that we hear; it is a homophonic universe. No wonder that Queneau expressed the desire to be a ventriloquist.

Here is a British critic, Martin Esslin, pushing the Entente Cordiale a bit far: 'Queneau's thought represents a point of inter-section between French existentialism on the one hand, and Anglo-Saxon linguistic philosophy on the other' (*23*, p. 79). It seems truer to say that Queneau, in philosophy as in all else, behaves as an eclectic, picking what best suits his purposes from different traditions of thought. Indeed, he can mock the very practice of philosophy, to the extent of giving the fairground voyeurs, in *Pierrot mon ami*, ogling the underwear on fleeting display at the hot-air machine, the name of *philosophes* (p. 105). In that same novel, Queneau's favourite philosopher of flux, Heraclitus, is somewhat brought down to earth, when his most famous paradox—that we can never step twice into the same river—is rendered thus: 'On ne se lave jamais deux fois les pieds dans la même flotte' (p. 167). And the famous *clarté* of the great seventeenth-century French philosopher, Descartes, is deflated when, in *Les Derniers Jours*, the projection of a stream of uncloudy urine is described as 'pisser de façon cartésienne' (p. 177).

To return to Esslin's remark about existentialism, it remains true that, in Queneau's most overtly 'philosophical' novel, *Le Chiendent*, its hero does gradually achieve (in Sartrian terms) *être-pour-soi* (i.e. he passes from unconscious vegetation to three-dimensional plenitude), and at the same time *être-pour-autrui* (when he becomes an object of observation to another person who follows him around). All of this happens when the said hero breaks his shell of habit and begins to think. Queneau attempted, in *Le Chiendent*, to write, in present-day colloquial French, a novel based on the famous proposition of Descartes: 'Cogito ergo sum': I think, therefore I am. As Esslin points out, however, for Descartes the phenomenon of human thought was the proof, and not the cause, of existence. G.-E. Clancier describes the three stages of this hero's existential development very neatly in these terms: (1) 'Je pense et je découvre que je suis.' (2) 'Je pense un peu plus et je ne sais plus qui je suis.' (3) 'Je pense plus encore et je ne sais plus si je suis' (*5*, p. 107). We seem to be drifting away from existentialism and Descartes into an older, and partly comic, tradition of uncertainty, self-doubt, scepticism. It is also the tradition of Ovid's *Metamorphoses*: magic changes occur in nearly all of Queneau's fictions. When Etienne Marcel, the hero of *Le Chiendent*, finally accepts that appearances can be deceptive ('On croit faire ceci et l'on fait cela. Toute action est déception, toute pensée implique erreur' (p. 223)), he is reabsorbed by his previous banality, and rebecomes flat, a commonplace common pleb. In *Les Derniers Jours*, a character says: 'On apprend les mots, mais les choses réelles

on ne les connaît pas. On sait des noms mais on ignore complète-
ment de quoi il s'agit' (p. 193). In the same novel there is a motif
of Einstein's Relativity Theory. We seem to be closing the circle
which leads back to the hilarious pyrrhonism (philosophical scepticism) of 'Pataphysics. But remember the splendid argument of
Etienne Marcel, taxed with scepticism: 'Ce n'est pas être sceptique
de détruire l'erreur, et quelle erreur plus grave que de croire savoir
ce qu'on ne sait pas?' (p. 163). *Errare humanum est.*

All this dubiousness makes Queneau very chary about laying
down the law on any matter. In his philosophical poem about the
evolution of the cosmos, *Petite cosmogonie portative*, Queneau
says at one point: 'Celui-ci voyez-vous n'a rien de didactique / que
didacterait-il sachant à peine rien?' (p. 128). In that same poem,
Queneau grants only two lines to human history ('Le singe (ou
son cousin) le singe devint homme / lequel un peu plus tard dés-
agrégea l'atome' (p. 162)). The remaining section of the poem is
devoted to the history of machines, ending with computers— though
of course we must concede that machines are human inventions.
Indeed, the poem as a whole celebrates the invention of forms.[2]
At the same time, the intention is obviously to puncture man's
pretentiousness, though in a typically oblique way. For me, one
of the best metaphorical expressions of Queneau's probable philosophy of life comes in *Le Chiendent*, where it is remarked of people
eating: 'Ils ne se doutaient pas que l'assiette pleine cachait une
assiette vide, comme l'être cache le néant' (p. 182). That is, it seems
to me that Queneau oscillates between different possibilities and
poles, now stressing the fullness and enjoyability of life, and then
sounding a more distressing note of something like angst. Like the
hero of *Les Derniers Jours*, no doubt Queneau too at times underwent 'un désespoir abominable dont le sortait brusquement un
optimisme tenace et dérisoire, un absurde goût de la vie' (p. 116).
Queneau was enough of his times, the generation of Sartre and
Camus, to offer an Absurdist view of life comparable to theirs, if
by no means identical.

---

[2] A high-powered computer at Euratom was nicknamed Zazie: Zahlen
Analyser Zuur Informazione Exploitation. This German/English/Dutch/
Italian/French conglomerate must have delighted the polyglot Queneau.

For Queneau's response to the absurd, to gratuitousness, is different from theirs. There is a well-known photo of Queneau wielding a broom, unless he is simply leaning on it, in the course of some fatigue during his military service. Later, he expressed the wish to be a street-sweeper. The hero of *Le Dimanche de la vie*, Valentin Brû, does latrine-duty cheerfully in the Army, leads a life of 'benign atheism', is hostile to evil, pain and aggressiveness on the part of his fellows, and aspires to be what we can only and rather unhelpfully call a saint. This goes with an urge to retreat, and to become transparent: to empty oneself of being, and thus to cease representing even a potential cause of suffering to other people. Valentin tries to keep a watch on Time, by emptying his head and gaping steadfastly at a public clock, but he can never quite experience Time in its pure state, uncontaminated by human associations. Similarly, vanity gets in the way of the urge to saint-liness, for him as for Jacques l'Aumône, the hero of *Loin de Rueil*. Another aspect of the same urge is the attraction felt by other Queneau heroes for the mechanical and the abstract: verbal games and mathematical puzzles. Furthermore, there are evident links between saintliness and idiocy, or at least mindlessness or vacancy. In other words: the fewer demands you make on life or on your brain-box, the less likely you are to be frustrated or to harm others. One final variation of this urge towards minimalism and depersonalisation (cf. 'Rien. Rien offre des avantages', in *Loin de Rueil* (p. 155)) is shown in that Jacques l'Aumône who manages, in his mania for the cinema, to translate himself on to the screen, to give himself a one-dimensional existence as a mythified film-star: the reverse process to that of Etienne Marcel in *Le Chiendent*.

In Queneau's special world, fools, or streamlined people, comment, often rudely, on the rest of mankind, also seen as fools, ignoramuses or otherwise defective. The net outcome of this pattern or equation is a mixture of authorial neutrality and gentle mockery at the folly of us all. As for his own activites, Queneau confessed that he liked the devising and the polishing stages of writing, but not the filling-in between. Hence perhaps those partly disincarnated heroes. In fact, witnessing the extremes of doubt operating in Queneau's fiction, we might be tempted to ask, with the American folk-philosopher Sylvester Allen: 'Is there a life before death?'

The one certainty in life, self-evidently, is death itself. *Les Derniers Jours* revolves entirely about the cycle of seasons, young students ageing and old people dying: all of them fretting or anguished about what one of Queneau's best collection of poems calls 'l'instant fatal'. The hero, the waiter Alfred, ends the book with an apocalyptic vision of a time when 'l'univers entier s'évanouira, ayant accompli son destin, comme ici et maintenant s'accomplit le destin des hommes' (p. 233). Until that dire day, we still need to occupy ourselves.

3 *Queneau: Games and structures*

With so much movement (or *play*) between reality and illusion, being and nothingness, plenitude and derealisation, we might well conclude (one of Queneau's unfavourite words, as it was for Flaubert), but for the evident preoccupation with death, that everything is 'only' a game for Queneau. If everything is essentially absurd, then the artist is freed to construct his own patterns of meaning. As Esslin puts it, grandiosely: 'In the face of the vast chaos that confronts us we can create small areas of order and symmetry like children building sand-castles on a beach lapped by the endless and formless ocean' (*23*, p. 85). Before talking about the patterns and structures of Queneau's fiction, whose innovations, by his own admission, owe much to the example of William Faulkner, I will discuss briefly the formal games he plays outside his novels. First of all, in a branch of the already mentioned 'Collège de 'Pataphysique', called the OULIPO ('*Ou*vroir de *litt*érature *po*tentielle'). This 'workshop' is based on the premiss that, in literature too, *do-it-yourself* can successfully function; that a ready-made literary text can be reconstituted to provide both recreation and re-creation; existing works can be recycled to make new works. As most true artists know very well, and Queneau better than most, plagiarism is creative. To this end, the members of this experimental group have applied all kinds of quite arbitrary methods to texts. For example, the 'S + 7' method, whereby each noun in a text is replaced by the seventh noun which follows it in a dictionary. Queneau, for one, admitted that some texts resist such approaches, but claimed that Genesis, for example, provided some good variations.[3] Another finding of the *Oulipiens* is that, by chopping off the rhyming sections of each line of a sonnet by Mallarmé and setting them down like a Japanese *haiku*, they not only produced a new poem but also made the meaning of the original poem clearer.

---

[3] See *Bâtons, chiffres et lettres*, pp. 336 et seq. My own experiment on the line 'When Rachel saw that she bare Jacob no children' gives 'bare Jehovah no chimpanzee'. It depends, naturally, on the dictionary you use.

This is because, in a tight form like the sonnet, the meaning is concentrated at the end of the line, in the rhyme. To the accusation that such games are purely artificial, Queneau responded, in his conversations with Georges Charbonnier, that nothing is more artificial than a sonnet or a five-act tragedy with its 'three unities' (p. 140). In *Bords*, Queneau likened creative work to the activity of a compiler of crossword-puzzles (p. 79). Queneau broke away from Surrealist circles quite soon, and there is certainly nothing Surrealistic in the games of the *Oulipiens*, which are designed to run counter to chance, and not to give chance a free hand. Lest the whole enterprise seemed excessively frivolous, Queneau was fond of pointing out that number-theory in advanced mathematics started out as a 'mere' game. One definition of the *Oulipiens*, in *La Littérature potentielle*, is : 'Rats qui ont à construire le laby-rinthe dont ils se proposent de sortir' (p. 36). They use self-built obstacles as trampolines or starting-blocks. A slightly perverse occupation, but honourable nonetheless, for amongst the ancestors of combinatorial art are Breughel the Elder, Leibniz and Mozart (p. 47).[4]

The other experimental venture occurs in the astounding booklet of ten sonnets, entitled *Cent mille milliards de poèmes*. Queneau took the initial idea from the children's game, called in French 'Têtes de rechange' or 'Têtes folles', in which successive pictures of bodies are cut laterally into three: head, torso and legs, which can then be rearranged to make bizarre combinations. In Queneau's hands, each of the 14 lines of each of the 10 sonnets can be per-mutated. This gives 10^{14} poems. If you read round the clock, you would have enough reading for nearly 200 million years. Thus we have the longest book in the world in only 10 pages. The reader is invited to be active, to make up his own sonnets from the possibili-ties. For, obviously, not only the reader but even the author himself has never read it through completely. For those who find such an approach to poetry repellent because calculating, Queneau replies in advance, in *Odile*: 'Le véritable inspiré . . . l'est toujours; il ne cherche pas l'inspiration, et ne s'irrite contre aucune technique'

---

[4] One of the *Oulipiens*, Georges Perec, wrote a 300-page novel without using the letter e, and composed a 5,000-word palindrome. (see *La Littérature potentielle*, p. 96 and pp. 101-6).

(p. 159). Queneau's classical preference for craft and graft over effusion is blatant here.

It often appears, nevertheless, that Queneau is mostly interested in purely formal matters, indeed in *exercices de style*. He has been claimed by certain critics to act as a kind of bridge between the traditional realist novel of the nineteenth-century and the 'Nouveau Roman' of Robbe-Grillet, Butor or Duras, with its far greater stress on structures, far more self-conscious approach to narration, and its hostility to traditional methods of characterisation. It is certainly true that *Le Chiendent*, as well as being an attempt to put the philosophy of Descartes into modern dress and present-day speech, was constructed on a mathematical basis, although its numerical patterns were dictated largely by personal fads: e.g. the number 7, because of the seven letters in Queneau's forename and surname.[5] He regulates the entrances and exits of his personages with great precision. He said, in *Bâtons, chiffres et lettres*, that he had never been able to see any real difference between novels and poems (p. 43). As a result, he continued, the writer of a novel can 'faire rimer des situations ou des personnages comme on fait rimer les mots; on peut même se contenter d'allitérations' (p. 42). Indeed, in all his novels, words or sentences recur as pointed refrains. Nearly all of his novels have a kind of circular shape, in which, after a great deal of agitation, the main character ends up more or less back at square one. It is the movement of return tickets, *aller-retour*, like the arrival in and departure from Paris of Zazie. Queneau evolved, however, from the early stage of arithmetical fixations, and broadened his scope to include linguistic variations of all kinds: 'Langage en tant que jeu avec des règles', Queneau defined it to Georges Charbonnier, 'disons un jeu de raisonnement, ou un jeu de hasard avec un maximum de raisonnement' (p. 56). All these items add up to what we could call disciplined anarchy, and Queneau's statement in the same text: 'Je n'ai pas toujours obéi à moi-même'

5 In *Voyage en Grèce* (p. 221), Queneau stated that he was equally obsessed at that period with J.W. Dunne's *An Experiment with Time*. The "observer" at the start of *Le Chiendent* was a figure borrowed by Dunne from Relativity Theory in order to explain premonitory dreams. Other influences on *Le Chiendent* are Heidegger and Husserl, and especially Plato's highly abstract *Parmenides*, which already contained possibly an element of parody.

(p. 54) shows how much of a temperamental anarchist he is, who does not like being bound by rules, even those of his own devising. Like all true anarchists, Queneau's fictional people are driven by obsessions, or rather by whims erected to the status of ambitions (think of Zazie's hunger for her 'blue-jeans'). The beasts they ride are always hobby-horses. Each character tends to pursue his or her own train of thought (and they often miss their connections) with sublime disregard for what anyone else is trying to say at the same moment. Queneau in fact complained to Georges Charbonnier that writers are too subject to the laws of linearity, i.e. words having to follow each other in Indian file, whereas often he himself would wish to juxtapose or to counterpoint events or dialogues (p. 13).

Just as he recommends greater freedom in the kinds of structures and the range of languages used in fiction, so Queneau has always been resolutely democratic in his attitude to subject-matter. In his *Petite cosmogonie portative*, he says: 'On parle du front des yeux du nez de la bouche / alors pourquoi pas de chromosomes pourquoi?' (p. 128). There is no hierarchy of subjects, or of values, for Queneau. He responds to all experience with the same alternation of wonderment and apprehension. He is a very even-handed, though hardly a serene, writer. 'Mes personnages sont souvent des simples d'esprit, dit-on. Je ne le pense pas du tout. Il faut être une bien grosse tête pour se permettre d'être méprisant', a rare admission for any writer, above all a French one, to make. Valentin Brû puts his refusal of disdain somewhat more scornfully, and perhaps honestly: 'Au nom de quelle supériorité se permettait-il de . . . se croire d'un degré au-dessus de ces paltoquets et de ces morveux?' (p. 234). Perhaps the best point of balance comes in *Pierrot mon ami*, where a character remarks of his fellow mortals: 'Sur une grande échelle, ça devient moche; à hauteur d'individu, c'est distrayant' (p. 185). As there is no hierarchy of subject-matter, some of Queneau's deeper concerns (death, filth and sexuality) are nearly always treated comically. For an Absurdist, death is the only undeniable reality. As for filth, Queneau admits in *Chêne et chien*: 'Certes j'avais du goût pour l'ordure et la crasse / images de ma haine et de mon désespoir' (p. 45). Thus, in *Les Enfants du limon*, Queneau treats us to a magnificent poem, outdoing Fungus the Bogeyman, on the disgusting habits of the obscene dwarf, Bébé-

Toutout (p. 33). As for sexuality, one of the few examples of the genuinely erotic book can be found in Queneau's *Oeuvres complètes de Sally Mara*, which is a homage to James Joyce, to the human body and all its vagaries ('phallucinations'), and to the languages we use to express our multitudinous desires. Its general theme of the linguistic and sexual apprenticeship of young girls links it with *Zazie dans le métro*.

If we attempted to find a global description for the denizens of Queneau's special but recognisable world, we might call them puppets. This would imply that the author is very securely, and even visibly, in charge of the whole proceedings. Or silhouettes, a word Queneau himself has favoured and quite aptly, as there is something rather phantom-like about many of his figures. Or counters, pawns. Here we would be acknowledging the game-element, the mathematical pattern-making. Queneau himself once confessed that for him the most important fact about his characters was not so much the actions the committed as the poetic climate in which they operated.[6] Climate, or perhaps *mood*. Perhaps it is not surprising that Queneau was a lifelong devotee of that mood-palace, the cinema, as he was of funfairs. In *Bâtons, chiffres et lettres*, he pointed out that the early cinema started in fact on fairgrounds and thus has a firm popular foundation. Fairgrounds and fleapits crop up regularly in Queneau's fiction. Despite the proximity of other bodies, cinemagoers, like readers of books, are essentially alone, face to face with their private dreams. Similarly, in Queneau's novels, we see people often in company, gangs, crowds, but, equally importantly, alone, musing, in a world of their own.

[6] In an interview 'La Poésie nue', *Journal des Poètes*, March 1952, p. 1.

4 Zazie dans le métro: *The war of words*

From various references in this novel to the Second World War and the Occupation of France, a reader might well deduce that *Zazie dans le métro* was probably started in the late 1940s, if not completed and published till 1959. For instance, Zazie's mother says 'Natürlich,' as she has been 'occupée' (and we can easily imagine her relationships with German soldiers) (p. 12). The counter in Turandot's bar (popularly known as *le zinc*) is often referred to as 'le zinc en bois depuis l'occupation' (because of the shortage of metal in those days). Gridoux saves his dog-ends, as he did during the Occupation (p. 77). Gabriel worked in Germany during the War, under the system of 'S.T.O.' (*Service de Travail Obligatoire*) (p.70). There is a flourishing business of American ex-army surplus and references to the Black Market. Finally, Gabriel goes in for lyrical nostalgia in claiming that he was never afraid during bombardments; indeed, he stayed above ground to watch the colourful explosions, while the yellow-belly German occupiers cowered in underground shelters. It was, he maintains, one hell of a spectacle (p. 38).

Queneau told Marguerite Duras that, in fact, the first few pages were written in 1945, and that he restarted work on the novel in 1953 (*22*, p. 28). One of his original ideas, he wrote in 1959, was to have a little girl, in league with her grandmother, robbing and killing mugs in the Métro corridors. Who would ever suspect this junior and this senior citizen, who would whoop it up on the proceeds? A variant idea was to have this pair engaged in a Homeric circumnavigation of the Métro-network; as they have only one ticket, they have to keep changing at *correspondances*, on their circular journey.[7] From the outset then, we have the notions of violence springing from an unexpected quarter, and constant locomotion.

Zazie dans le métro can be read, simply, as a comic adventure-

[7] See Queneau: 'Zazie dans son plus jeune âge', *Les Lettres Nouvelles*, 2, March 1959, pp. 5-7.

story. But, just as its people enjoy chewing the fat, so the reader may find, if he probes, a good deal of lean, and even some of that 'substantial marrow' that Rabelais, one of Queneau's masters, promised in *Gargantua*. *Zazie* is the best introduction to Queneau's fictional world. Not so riddled with philosophical speculation as *Le Chiendent*, more tied to the everyday, non-mythical universe than *Saint-Glinglin*, funnier than *Pierrot mon ami* or *Les Fleurs bleues*, it is the most approachable of his works, even if none of them is immediately assimilable without some effort on the part of the reader.

'Doukipudonktan?' (p. 9) (*D'où qu'ils puent donc tant?*). This first sentence, compressed phonetically into one continuous word, hints that this novel will be primarily concerned with language: its plasticity, its oddities, its mechanisms and conventions. Now, obviously, all literature, and a good deal of life, depends on language. The wordless book has yet to be written. But obsession with language clearly varies in degree from one writer to another. Queneau belongs to that wing of writers whose principal interest lies in words. Now, this does not mean that he is uninterested in philosophy, politics, history, or even the observation and reproduction of ordinary human behaviour. He was a man and he had human interests. But language comes first among these.

One of the first, and most frequently recurring, uses of language in this novel is for insult, the exchange of, as we say quaintly in English, 'personal remarks'. Together with curiosity about other people (see Gridoux's obsessive questions about *le type* on pp. 70-1), in *Zazie dans le métro* insult is the commonest mode of addressing a fellow mortal. People here constantly speak to each other in terms which forcefully suggest that the other person has interstellar space between his two ears, or that he or she is somewhat deficient in personal hygiene or in some vital component of sexual equipment. Now, the foreign, especially Anglo-Saxon, visitor to France is often struck by the impression that everyone there is quarrelling with everyone else. People strike attitudes, opinionate at the drop of a hat, stick to their guns, counter-attack, or refuse even to listen to contrary arguments. In fact, of course, this phenomenon is part of the rich tapestry of French (and all Latin) social intercourse. From our own society, however, we have only to remember the

normal fashion of discourse between close friends, often grounded
on cheerful denigration and deflation. On the very first page of
Zazie dans le métro, we get smell and counter-smell, leading swiftly
on to insult and repartee. And, of course, hectoring is a stock
ingredient of several types of humour. Think of *Alice in Wonderland*,
and how rude everybody is to each other, of the Goons or Monty
Python, where John Cleese's whole dramatic and comic persona is
based on the temperament of a man who can barely contain his
anger at the inexplicable behaviour of his fellow-men. In *Zazie*,
we see not only the ever-ready affront, but the instant cave-in,
still expressed in words, e.g. the 'verbal shield' which the little man
tries to interpose between himself and the menacing Gabriel. In
fact, as Gabriel raises his arm, the shrimp collapses to the ground.

A variation on insult occurs when a character sarcastically punc-
tures another person's boast. When Gabriel's alleged heroism during
the War is being extolled, Trouscaillon asks maliciously whether
he used to catch bombs in his open arms to stop them exploding.
And even the mild Madeleine, wondering what makes other women
more special to her beloved Charles than she herself appears to be,
asks whether perhaps they have 'le baba en or' (p. 76).[8] Sometimes
the string of imprecations can be self-deflating, anti-climactic, as
when Zazie refers to Trouscaillon as 'a loafer, an idiot, and even
. . . a Sunday-driver' (p. 66). (We will see later Zazie's own particular and perhaps more characteristic brand of verbal sadism.)
Nevertheless, despite all the insults which pepper this novel,
physical, as distinct from verbal, violence is pretty scarce until
the chaotic grand finale. Gabriel, for instance, is usually reluctant
to exploit his considerable physical strength unless really provoked.
In that scene at the station with the obstreperous little man, Gabriel
expresses regret at the predominance of violence in human affairs
since the beginning of social living, but concludes 'philosophically'
that it is not his fault if it is always little squirts who get up your
nose. Later on, after heaving the obnoxious pest Trouscaillon down
the stairs, Gabriel wonders whether he should invite him to lunch
(p. 72). On the other hand, the largely gentle Veuve Mouaque can
be roused to at least spoken aggression, by the unhelpful behaviour

[8]   A gold-plated pudendum.

of the manager in the tourist restaurant. She recommends that his (as they say in 'Monty Python') 'naughty bits' be twisted, so as to teach him a lesson (p. 132). But, in stressing the violence in this novel, let us never forget, too, the frequent joviality and comradeship expressed in eating and drinking together and in mutual help.

5 Gabriel, Zazie and Trouscaillon

Though hardly 'characters' in the traditional sense, the personages of this novel are given idiosyncrasies and thus a kind of differentiation. This 'depth', such as it is, occurs mostly in Gabriel and Zazie, and, by his multiplicity of guises, in Trouscaillon. Gabriel is typified by incongruousness. There is in him an ever-present gap between his desire to hide something and to show off, and between his lowly social status and confused intellect and the kind of ambitious statements he often utters. Though of enormous size (a 'wardrobe'), he is a man of some sensitivity, indeed fastidiousness. His perfume is 'Barbouze de Fior'; if *Fior* is a twist on Christian Dior, *un barbouze* is a bodyguard for a high official, a gorilla. Gabriel has a permanent urge to strike an impressive repertoire of poses, and to outdo other people by the vigour and the stylishness of his speeches. Just as popular speech, by being granted unlimited entry, is given here a new dignity, so Gabriel, who is sexually and vocationally 'marginal', constantly strives, with the willing help of his author, to ennoble himself. He refers to his calling (dressing up as a lady flamenco dancer or performing the Dying Swan in a tutu) as a choreographic art, and describes it as the principal udder of his income (p. 151). His extensive range of gestures Queneau usually leaves unspecified, thereby inviting the reader to fill in the details. Gabriel has an abiding concern for the nuances of language. Altogether, and perfectly naturally, given his profession, he is a showman. He is prone to 'philosophise' at the slightest opportunity, when, as Queneau puts it derisively, his 'Thomism' acquires 'Kantian' overtones (p. 13). This rather abstruse joke depends on the contrast between what we already know of Gabriel and the unlikeliness of his ever having even heard of St Thomas Aquinas or Immanuel Kant, who are in any case pretty strange bedfellows: one the great medieval theologian and the other a key figure of the eighteenth-century rationalist Enlightenment.[9] Throughout, Gabriel's would-be serenity and

---

[9] There is a similar joke about Veuve Mouaque being a mixture of budding passion for Trouscaillon and 'cartésianisme natif'—again the reference to Descartes, the great exponent of French rationalism (p. 116).

conciliatoriness are pitted against Zazie's constant state of rage. Generally, in fact, she is much too quick for him, either in her movements or in her mental gymnastics and her richly obscene language. Gabriel alternates between pride in his special talents as a *danseuse de charme*, and a touchy evasiveness, as when he lets Zazie believe for some time that he is a night-watchman, which would explain his sleeping in the day.

In *Le Chiendent*, a character muses: 'Ça lui apprendrait à prendre tout ce qui vient pour argent comptant. Il n'y a pas d'argent comptant, il n'y a que de fictives opérations de banque' (p. 224). One of the recurrent themes of *Zazie dans le métro* also is the unreliability of appearances, and this applies above all to Gabriel. He asserts that, even if he does perform an act in drag in a queers' night-club, that does not imply anything about his own sexuality. As Gridoux says: it is a job like any other (p. 79), or, as the proverb has it: 'Il n'y a point de sot métier'. Both have a point. Gabriel claims to provide entertainment for his customers precisely because he is so huge. That is, the disproportion between what he is dressed up to appear—a very feminine woman—and what he is—a colossal male—is inherently comic. The audience, he says proudly, wets itself laughing at his act (p. 63). But he goes further. 'Y a pas que la rigolade. Y a aussi l'art' (p. 167). He sees himself as a kind of angel-figure, 'édénique et adamique'. He slips in this self-estimate in the middle of a lyrical barker's patter about the lovely lolly ('this mellifluous, savoury and multi-creative product' (p. 151)) he earns from his artistic performances. 'J'ai oint la jointure de mes genoux avec ladite sueur de mon front': it is not only a question of art but also of hard work. This speech is also a kind of joky manifesto for the exploited of the earth, from Adam and Eve onwards, who were so harshly treated, as was the Serpent, by the Elohim. The anti-religious tone is pronounced ('Biblical balls'). He goes on to explain his substitute credo: 'L'art' (a four-letter word for Gabriel) is infinitely superior to the three or five-letter words (i.e. *con* and *merde*) which so frequently bespatter French speech. To back up his argument, he executes a few *entrechats* with his hands fluttering behind his back to simulate the flight of a butterfly (p. 152). He is indeed a kind of winged creature. He is instantly adopted by the foreign tourists as a supplementary

guide, or *archiguide*—which suggests perhaps, as does his name
Gabriel, an archangel (p. 96). *Ange*, in slang, can mean a homosexual, and, if Gabriel is indeed an angel, we can of course debate
eternally about his true gender. All in all, unlike several of Queneau's
strangely innocent heroes, Gabriel is not a pre-Adamite figure, but
he is all the more interesting for not quite qualifying.

Gabriel delivers two major speeches, the first at the foot of the
Eiffel Tower.[10] It starts off with a mixture of references to
Shakespeare's *Hamlet* and to the chief philosophical treatise of
Jean-Paul Sartre: 'L'être ou le néant, voilà la question' (pp. 90-1).
The speech is a madcap vision full of clichés, borrowed lyricism,
twists on familiar sayings. The only constants are the themes of
human frenzy and the inevitability of death. Looking forward to
Les Fleurs bleues where two men dream each other up, Gabriel
brings in the Spanish Golden Age playwright Calderón and his con-
cept of 'Life is a Dream', and the famous proposition from *Macbeth*
about life being a tale told by an idiot, full of sound and fury,
signifying nothing. This is Gabriel's version (and notice how
Queneau works in a dig against himself as the perpetrator): 'Gabriel
n'est qu'un rêve (charmant), Zazie le songe d'un rêve (ou d'un
cauchemar), et toute cette histoire le songe d'un songe, le rêve d'un
rêve, à peine plus qu'un délire tapé à la machine par un romancier
idiot (oh! pardon)'. The implication is that, if all of his creations
are barmy, then so is their creator (God, or Queneau). Gabriel also
hints at Falstaff and the key imperative of keeping alive ('Mais moi
je suis vivant et là s'arrête mon savoir'). It is a reiterative, strongly
rhythmic discourse. And it does not aim to prove the impossibility
of human communication, as it might in a play by Beckett or
Ionesco. Rather, it is as if the reshuffling of commonplaces and
truisms could still beget a peculiar kind of poetry. Gabriel says,
in a pure Alexandrine: 'Les voilà presque morts puisqu'ils sont des
absents' (p. 91): a stylish variation on 'Out of sight, out of mind'.
(Indeed, he is truly concerned for Zazie only when she is in his
purview.) The speech is in fact an inverted burlesque. Traditional
burlesque gives low language to highborn people. Queneau here
does the reverse. The intention is not to destroy, but to loosen

[10] In the excellent film of the novel, directed by Louis Malle, he makes the
speech even more appropriately standing on top of a lift ascending the Tower.

constraints, to widen the scope of literature. Gabriel's perorations are clearly rhetorical in character, attention-seeking. (Similarly, Turandot *acts* despair, making the futile show of pulling off his own head in anguish (p. 21)).

The second speech takes place on the terrace of the café des Deux Palais (p. 117). Again, we hear echoes of *Hamlet*, and of the seventeenth-century French thinker Pascal ('le silence des espaces infinis'). This time, Gabriel mixes into his pseudo-philosophical *spiel* about the fragility and uncertainty of human existence some showman's puff which serves as a plug for his night-club act. Once more, the comedy resides in the contrast of a beefy man in a tutu speculating on the oldest and thorniest problems of philosophy: death and human impermanence. Later, he makes jokes about the whole question of human freedom. Whereas Trouscaillon and Veuve Mouaque think that he has been kidnapped, Gabriel himself feels that he has in fact turned the tables on his abductors to such an extent that he is now in control of their free-will, and they have become his slaves (p. 118). Beneath all this joking and verbal play, there runs a serious idea, even though it is expressed risibly. It is that the precarious nature of human life, its vulnerability, makes us better able to put up with the mis-fortunes and sufferings we have to bear. Even if everything is absurd, there are salvageable *petits bonheurs*. 'Value the fragility of it all' is Queneau's message, if he were capable of such a monstrosity!

Gabriel says at one point that he only ever speaks in generalisa-tions: 'Je ne fais pas de demi-mesures' (p. 176). One such is his pedagogical theory about the bringing-up of children, which he maintains should be founded on 'la compréhension' (p. 100). And this is where Zazie makes her rowdy entrace. We should keep in mind that, in this novel, relations between child and grown-ups are presented largely in burlesque fashion, but, remembering Queneau's psycho-analytic treatment, we may wonder whether this account represents a triumphing over some deep-seated anxieties on this score.

There were prototypes of Zazie already in earlier novels like *Un Rude Hiver*: acidulous, sexually inquisitive but still childish young girls. For Queneau himself, Zazie is eleven or twelve years old, a nymphet, as Nabokov's *Lolita* taught us to say. Like her uncle

Gabriel, she is built of contrasts: a little girl with a foul mouth and curiosities which are supposed to be beyond her age, although Freud argued that children from the earliest age are intensely sexual, in a variety of bewildering ways, which he called 'the polymorphous perverse'. And, periodically, she reverts to type, for example crying when she finds that the Métro she so much wanted to visit is on strike. She takes this situation personally: 'Ah, les vaches. Me faire ça à moi', she exclaims (p. 12). We first see her being handed over to the tender negligence of Gabriel by a mother who makes the barest pretence of maternal solicitude: she tells Gabriel that she does not want Zazie to be raped by the entire family, a juicy foretaste of the later horror-story recounted by Zazie about her father.

Zazie's roles in this novel are: (a) to comment, nearly always rudely, on all that happens or is said to her or around her. Perhaps her most notorious comment occurs when Napoleon is mentioned, and she says: 'Napoléon mon cul. Il m'intéresse pas du tout, cet enflé, avec son chapeau à la con' (p. 16). (b) to ask awkward questions, as when she aggressively says to Gabriel: 'Quand tu déconnes comme ça, tu le fais exprès ou c'est sans le vouloir?' (p. 17). (*Question* in French has a useful ambiguity, for it also means torture, as in *mettre à la question*). No wonder Charles complains that Zazie makes his brain ache with all her leading queries, which give him vertigo, a dangerous state to be in half-way up the Eiffel Tower (p. 89). Zazie has come up to the capital from the provinces. Queneau is using the device, particularly popular in French eighteenth-century literature, of introducing a Stranger, here a child provincial, into a society in order to criticise it and to wreak havoc. Her information is based on snippets gathered from local newspapers, television, cinema, and her Bible, the Memoirs of General Vermot.[11] An example of her bitty knowledge is shown when she enquires insultingly of Charles whether he found his clapped-out taxi on the banks of the River Marne—a reference to a famous event in World War I when Paris taxis were used *en masse* to transport troops in that sector. (c) Zazie represents 'the younger generation', always

[11] Queneau is here referring to the Almanach Vermot, a popular annual specialising in stereotyped cartoons, nuggets of supposed folk wisdom, offers of magic talismans, and atrocious puns. Its attitudes are typically reactionary.

a source of consternation to its elders. As for her name, Queneau has explained that (as well as being a familiar form of Isabelle) it is derived from the *zazous*, who were a section of the postwar adolescent generation fond of dressing American-style and of jazz. They were usually regarded as delinquent by their families and by right-thinking society at large. Zazie, said Queneau, is the daughter of the *zazous* (*22*, p. 27).

An American definition of the child is: 'A stomach surrounded entirely by curiosity'. Zazie is governed by imperious obsessions: (1) to see and to ride on the Paris Métro. (2) To acquire some blue-jeans (spelt *djinns bleus* at one point. Djinns, in Mohammedan lore, were good *or* bad spirits). (3) To find out whether her uncle Gaby is or is not *un hormosessuel*. (4) To find out what this word means. (5) Generally, like any child (and most adults), to get her own way. As Roland Barthes points out, she speaks only in the imperative or optative moods, i.e. 'Gimme' or 'I want' (*15*, p. 678). And (6) She has an ambition to be a teacher, so that she can 'faire chier les mômes'. Gloatingly, she details how she will treat her charges: she'll make them lick the floor, eat the blackboard sponge; she'll stick compasses in their buttocks and boot their backsides with spurs on (p. 24). Gabriel's response is bland. He says he thought that modern education was progressing in a different direction, towards gentleness and understanding. When he goes on to forecast that teachers will soon be supplanted by machines, Zazie counters by declaring that, in that case, she will become an astronaut instead, 'pour aller faire chier les Martiens'. No wonder they are bug-eyed at the prospect. Later, with *le type* (i.e. Trouscaillon), she assures him that, if he is had up in court on a morals charge, for which he will certainly be guillotined, she will personally collect his severed head from the sawdust basket and spit on it (p. 66). Gabriel nearly faints at the mention of such atrocities. Is her sadism just childish boasting, talking big? Not entirely. She kicks Gabriel's ankle and savagely nips his fleshy thighs, when he refuses to answer her pointblank questions (p. 97). Rather than give her a thump which might dislodge some teeth and, incidentally, lose him the favour of his group of tourist admirers, he puts up with his punishment stoically, 'en assumant son martyre', again revealing his angelic aspect (p. 103). In a nice twist on the more usual sort of scene, a passing lady tells

Zazie off for beating up a grown-up (p. 100). Her importunate
questions are 'too old' for Charles (p. 92). It is a topsy-turvy world
in *Zazie dans le métro*.

When Zazie tells her dreadful story of her drunkard, rapist
father, eventually murdered by her mother with the complicity
of her fancy-man of the moment, a butcher, it is clear that Zazie
positively enjoys the narration. Like Gabriel, she is a born performer,
and she revels in her own oral inventiveness, and in keeping her
audience, Trouscaillon, on tenterhooks (p. 53). What is more, she
relishes the spectacle within the spectacle. When her raving father
starts rolling his eyes and locking the door, she remembers thinking
that it was a stupendous sight, just like at the pictures. Zazie, indeed,
seems to be more sympathetic towards her father than towards the
avenging mother, perhaps because the father was at least acting
sincerely in lusting after his own daughter, whereas the mother
put on a hypocritical performance in doing in the man she wanted
to get rid of, anyway, for her own selfish purposes. Ironically,
though the mother got off with a verdict of justifiable homicide,
the butcher then started hovering around Zazie—a magnet for
several men in this book—and so the mother had to throw him
out, complaining that she could not kill them all, or people might
begin to talk. Zazie has her narcissistic side. Dressed in her skin-
tight jeans, gazing at herself in a mirror, 'elle passa ses mains sur ses
petites fesses, moulées à souhait et perfection, et soupira profondé-
ment, grandement satisfaite' (p. 63). As Gabriel comments: 'Il y a
des amateurs' (p. 120).[12]

Queneau says paradoxically of Zazie at one point: 'Elle file
droit devant elle en zigzag' (p. 56). When it comes to interpretation,
she is a moving target. She herself is somewhat unisex, not unlike her
uncle; a caracter seeing her in her jeans thinks she is 'déguisée en
garçon' (p. 112). She is not a single representative of anything,
except of desire, and desire is morally ambivalent. She does not
stand for Truth, for her father-story is possibly pure fabrication

[12] Yvonne, in *Pierrot mon ami*, going through a similar ceremonial of loving self-
inspection, is admired by the author, marvelling at her 'joie d'elle-même'
(p. 85). A lovely tribute from this least porcinely chauvinistic of men.

or exaggeration. Her *petite voix intérieure* has something of the devil in it. Various characters say of her, wonderingly: 'Elle a de la suite dans les idées', by which they mean not so much logic as mule-like obstinacy (p. 103). Even when she cries, she makes sure that she gets some mileage from her tears. As she remains a child through thick and thin, the snotty face down which her tears course runs with muddy rivulets (p. 45). All in all, she refuses to be overawed by the would-be confident behaviour and words of looming adults: she is the anti-dupe. She is ferocious and voracious, and at one point, while devouring shellfish, she is likened to a cannibal (p. 51). She refuses sentiment. She loathes happy endings in films, and prefers it when everyone is killed off in the last reel. As Veuve Mouaque comments sadly: 'Les enfants, c'est bien connu. Ça n'a pas de coeur' (p. 176). Zazie is light-years away from the monstrously good children of Enid Blyton, or Saint-Exupéry's Petit Prince, who talks to roses and carries one lovingly about with him. Zazie has been compared to a cocky ventriloquist's dummy, deflating the pretentiousness and respectability of its master. While she generally gets her own way, or at least successfully resists the wishes of her elders and betters (or worsers), there are times when the worms turn and an anti-Zazie movement is at least contemplated. For instance, weary of her questioning and ill-treatment of Gabriel, his fans toss up whether to throw Zazie in the Seine, or to wrap her in a travelling-rug with cotton-wool stuffed into her mouth so as to soundproof her, and then to deposit her in a left-luggage office. If nobody were willing to give up a rug, a suitcase would do, as long as they stuffed her into it tightly (p. 119). In fact, in the concluding frenetic section, Zazie is sporadically sleepy and hardly takes part in or comments on the action, though she is conscious enough to express some admiration at last for uncle Gabriel after his epic battle with the café-waiters (p. 181). Until that point, she remains a baleful, almost diabolical presence, and, quite fittingly, Zazie is attracted to the 'demonic' Trouscaillon, who makes a suitable pendant to the 'angelic' Gabriel.

This weird character rejoices in various aliases: Pédro-Surplus (*le type*, who claims to run a clothes-stall in the flea-market), Trouscaillon (the policeman disguise), Bertin Poirée (his police-inspector role), and finally Aroun Arachide, at which point he

at last confesses his multiplicity of parts.[13] In fact, on his very first
appearance, he strikes Zazie, with his dark glasses, bowler-hat,
umbrella (*le pébroque*: *La Maison Pébroque* is slang for the Police,
or a blind for illegal activities), and his false moustache (*bacchantes*,
an apt accoutrement for this sex-mad creature) as an itinerant actor.
Referred to only as *le type* for most of his initial appearance, he
feigns at one point loss of identity. He has forgotten his name, he
maintains, as he never learnt it off by heart (p. 81). Until his final
speech, he gives away very little about himself. He offers a parody
of a potted autobiography (and Queneau, with his professed loathing
for interviews and questionnaires, would feel kinship with him on
this score): 'Je ne vous dirai rien de mon enfance ni de ma jeunesse.
De mon éducation, n'en parlons point. . . Célibataire depuis mon plus
jeune âge, la vie m'a fait ce que je suis' (p. 165). A perfect example
of using words to keep meaning at bay. Whereas Gabriel never varies
his professional act, Trouscaillon is in a constant state of versatility
(p. 166).[14] Despite often appearing to have sinister designs on the
other characters, even Trouscaillon (like the not very articulate
Madeleine, who manages the odd poignant remark)[15] has his
moments of solitary melancholy and longing for a different and less
encumbered style of life; he envies the *clochards* asleep on the
Métro-vents.[16] He too can meditate on the fragility of all things
and, like Robert Burns, on the ways in which "the best laid schemes
o' mice and men gang aft agley" (p. 162).

---

[13] *Trousser*: to womanise; *une caille*: a fast woman. *Poirée*: a sugar-beet;
Bertin Poirée: the name of a Paris street. *Arachide*: peanut; Aroun
Arachide: Haroun al-Rashid, hero of *The Arabian Nights*.

[14] 'Les artisses . . . Une fois qu'ils ont trouvé un truc, ils l'esploitent à fond.
Faut reconnaître qu'on est tous un peu comme ça, chacun dans son genre'
(p. 166). Possibly a self-jibe by Queneau here.

[15] 'Quelle colique que l'egsistence' (p. 145), with its twin suggestions of
mélancolique and of life running away from us. *Egsistence* is phonetically
more faithful than *existence*. cf. *Saint-Glinglin*, and variant spellings: *aigue-
sistence* (the watery life of fishes); *aigresistence*: the bitterness of life, etc.

[16] Perhaps the nearest that any of the more plenitudinous creatures of *Zazie
dans le métro* ever get to the honed-down existence of other Queneau
heroes. Similarly, there is here none of that recurrent urge towards saintliness, except, in parodic fashion, in the polarity of the archangel Gabriel
and the diabolical Trouscaillon.

When dressed as a policeman, he is taken by two real bicycle cops (*les hanvélos*) for a priest in disguise, which incites them to embark on a disquisition about secret conspiracies to link the Church and the Police: *le goupillon* (the holy-water sprinkler, often used as a symbol of the Catholic Church and, in slang, the penis) and *le bâton blanc*, symbol of the *flic* kingdom. Despite being arrested, Trouscaillon reappears later in his ultimate and climactic guise as Aroun Arachide, and utters these words: 'Je suis je, celui que vous avez connu et parfois mal reconnu. Prince de ce monde et de plusieurs territoires connexes' (p. 185). These words parody those attributed to Satan by St John the Evangelist. Aroun Arachide claims that his essence is variability, that he sows uncertainty and error all about him. But just how satanic is he? He is granted a comparison with Mephistopheles (p. 66), but, to me, he is more reminiscent of another trouble-maker, Protos, in Gide's *Les Caves du Vatican*. Protos was in turn modelled on the mythological figure of Proteus, who was forever changing his appearance. Trouscaillon's role is clearly one of metamorphosis; he creates layers of illusion. It is reminiscent of the role of Isis in Apuleius' *Golden Ass*, already evoked in *Le Chiendent*, who boasts of similar multi-faceted dominion over the whole world (see 7, p. 22). But then Trouscaillon admits that he failed as a policeman ('policier primaire et défalqué') (p. 185). So that, like Purpulan in *Les Enfants du limon*, he is perhaps more of a *pauvre diable* than a true demon. At one stage, when people are unsure whether he is a policeman or *un satyre* (a dirty old man), he is described in these self-cancelling terms: 'C'était pas un satyre qui se donnait l'apparence d'un faux flic, mais un vrai flic qui se donnait l'apparence d'un faux satyre qui se donne l'apparence d'un vrai flic' (p. 59). With Trouscaillon, we can watch how Queneau makes words generate new realities. Called *un flic* and *un satyre*, Trouscaillon becomes both in turn, as if summoned to do so. It is what he calls 'le métier de l'enveloppe' (p. 163).

I suspect that it is primarily the figure of Trouscaillon that made Roland Barthes, the fashionable guru of French literature, put so much stress, in his study of this novel, on negativity as its mainspring.[17]

17 See the Conclusion.

6 Satire, ethics and eroticism

One aspect of the comedy in this novel which is more straight-forward is the splendid satire of the tourist-trade, if we make due allowance for comic inflation. The tone of the guide, Fédor Balanovitch, is one of continuous insult.[18] He relies on the fact that his colourful string of French obscenities is Double Dutch (or, as the French say, Hebrew) to the motley gang of foreign tourists that he ferries around Paris at great speed. They are supposed to follow a clockwork itinerary ('Gibraltar aux anciens parapets' the next day). 'Package-tour' assumes its full meaning here, and they are taken for a ride in every sense of the term. Even Gabriel joins in rooking them by diverting them to a restaurant where he will pocket a rake-off. There the tourists gaze starry-eyed at all the 'local colour'—the waiters in long white aprons like sarongs, and the exquisite French cuisine: a filthy sauerkraut with mouldy bacon, sprouting potatoes and rancid ham (p. 130). Zazie takes one mouth-ful and announces out loud that the food provided is 'de la merde'. In this scene, Queneau clearly enjoys himself, mocking the French heritage, especially the Gauls, those ancestors so frequently evoked in France, who bequeathed to the French 'les braies, la tonnellerie et l'art non-figuratif' (p. 130). After Zazie's complaint, the manager, in typical Gallic fashion, i.e. by savage counter-attack, begins in-sulting the assembled horde, accusing them of effrontery and bar-baric ignorance: 'Tas de feignants, tandis que vous pratiquiez encore le cannibalisme en suçant la moelle des os de vos ennemis charcutés, nos ancêtres les Croisés préparaient déjà le biftèque pommes frites' (p. 132). This is an excellent rendering of French xenophobic reflexes. For her part, Zazie is mollified only by the manager's insidious offer of corned beef, and his promise to open the tin in front of her (p. 134). Altogether, the satire of tourism is the

---

[18] Balanovitch: son of the *balan*, or gland, a truly tautologous name!

satire of conducted tours, and Zazie sees more when she lets herself loose on the highways and byways than when she is supposedly shown round Paris by Gabriel and Charles. This pair of pontificating zanies confuse the Panthéon with the Gare de Lyon, and Les Invalides with an army barracks (p. 15). Such mistakes, of course, scratch lightly at the dignity of famous buildings and monuments. On similar ground, I particularly relished Gabriel's query as to why Paris is always thought of as feminine, when it has an elongated, erect phallic symbol, the Eiffel Tower, stuck down at its middle (p. 89).

In this often ambivalent novel, we may wonder who exactly corrupts whom. I am thinking of Turandot, proprietor of the bar 'La Cave' and of Gabriel's flat, complaining of Zazie's bad language in these choice terms: 'Merde de merde, je veux pas dans ma maison d'une petite salope qui dise des cochoncetés comme ça' (p. 21). When he attempts to stop Zazie doing a bunk, he soon attracts a crowd of critical bystanders, described ironically as 'moralistes sévères' (p. 34). In fact, as soon as Zazie begins inventively accusing Turandot of having sexual designs on her, the crowd of 'censors' becomes titillated and hungry for all the lurid details. In addition, of course, Queneau himself script-teases the reader at this point by taunting him or her with snippets of information, which increases the prurience of the scene. At a later stage, the tables are turned (inversion or reversal are Queneau's favourite operations): Trouscaillon accuses Zazie of theft, just in time to stall her from trying the same stunt of crying rape. We hear then a similar chorus of idle spectators, mouthing clichés like 'la propriété, c'est sacré' (p. 58). It is the voice of collective mindlessness, best typified by the impersonal pronoun *on*. On a gentler level, Veuve Mouaque retains 'des débris de moralité, pour les autres, dans les ruines de la sienne' (p. 129). Don't we all? In the main, just as Queneau refuses hierarchies of values, so he tends also not to work in any rigid ethical categories. His world is marked by tolerance, acceptance, which does not necessarily rule out a firm critical sense. And the fact that Queneau takes such a keen interest in formal matters does not abolish the possibility that, by trying to reform our awareness of language, he hopes also to affect our moral perceptions. In *Bâtons, chiffres et lettres*, he mentions the Chinese Emperor who, in order to transform public morals, started by changing the ideograms of the Chinese language (pp. 51 and 55).

Apart from Gabriel's efforts towards philosophy, the nearest this novel gets to seriousness comes in four scenes of differently sexual character. First of all, the scene between Zazie and *le type* (Trouscaillon) which leads up to his buying her the longed-for blue-jeans. It is a very good development, full of reciprocal play-acting and mutual mistrust. However absorbed Trouscaillon is in his new prey, he retains enough presence of mind to ask the American ex-army surplus stall-holder whether they had eleven-year old girls in the U.S. forces, as the jeans fit Zazie perfectly (p. 49). Zazie herself plays a very risky game with Trouscaillon throughout, telling herself not to trust him an inch as he is most probably one of the dirty raincoat brigade, but pulled ever onwards by her lust for the jeans he might be persuaded to buy her (p. 50).

Secondly, a rather more tenderly erotic fragment when Veuve Mouaque and Trouscaillon, walking along side by side in silence, gradually realise that they are indeed walking along, side by side, in silence. It puts a different cast on all the games with language played in the rest of the novel, for here the implication is that, even though human discourse is frequently nonsense, there are times when words are superfluous, anyway (p. 124). Naturally, Queneau is still mocking them, but it is here a minuscule mickey-take, a fond tease. Like Gabriel in his set-pieces, they achieve a kind of low-grade lyricism.

The third incident is a *scène troublante* between Madeleine and Marceline, whom we still believe at this point to be a female, conned by her clothes, and the adverb *doucement* which accompanies everything she does or says.[19] It is only on the very last page that 'she' is revealed to be a Marcel. Her relationship with Gabriel thus features a criss-cross transvestism. By concealing the sexual identity until the end (although the use of masculine nouns in the preceding pages—*le lampadophore*, *le manipulateur*—offers unnoticed clues), Queneau is questioning our stock responses. If we had known all along, we would have had a different, and possibly derisive, attitude to Gabriel and him/her. Troublingly, then, the scene with Madeleine

---

[19] In *L'Immoraliste* by Gide, who also hovered between the two sexes, the long-suffering wife is called 'la douce Marceline'.

is very tender, ultra-feminine, intimate, full of stillness and expectancy (p. 143).

A fourth scene, with both participants in disguise (one in drag and the other in police-inspector garb), features Marceline again, this time threatened with seduction by Bertin Poirée (i.e. Trouscaillon), who runs through a whole repertoire of what he believes to be bullying, then charm,—none of which has any effect whatsoever on the resourceful Marceline (pp. 155-61). In none of these scenes does Queneau openly take sides or intimate any ethical preferences. Nor does he in the case of poor mixed-up Charles, who spends much of his time not earning a living but mooning about over his matrimonial dilemmas. He has spent years searching for a soul-mate via the columns of a lonely-hearts magazine, but has been repeatedly disappointed, as the correspondents invariably strike him as stupid, lying or potentially bitchy (p. 13). As a result, he stays permanently on guard, keeping Madeleine (Mado P'tits Pieds) somewhat at bay, although they hop into bed together, so to speak, occasionally on the back staircase. Even when *le marida* is finally agreed, Charles feels that nothing will really be changed, except that they will henceforth be able to consummate their desires 'dans la légalité' (p. 139).

7 Laverdure and language

The moment has come to leave the personages in peace for a while and to return to my original proposition, from which I have never really strayed far: that this novel is primarily concerned with language. This will involve much enumeration but cataloguing is an essential element of any study of Queneau's humour and indeed an integral part of that humour itself.

The one 'character' I have not so far mentioned, Laverdure, the sombre and antisocial parrot belonging to Turandot, acts as a useful lead-in to the language question. Parrots were once defined as 'the only creatures with the power of speech that are content to repeat what they hear without trying to exaggerate it'. Queneau himself remarked on Laverdure's role: 'Dès que les gens commencent à envelopper ce qu'ils disent, à "mettre la sauce", c'est le rappel à l'ordre' (22, p. 27). For, by his refrain ('Tu causes, tu causes, c'est tout ce que tu sais faire' (passim)), he of course functions as an ironic commentator on the gabbling parrot-talk, or psittacism, of the human race: a favourite area also of writers like Beckett and Ionesco. At times, as if by contamination—psittacosis, or parrot-disease, can of course be transmitted to humans—some of the people take up Laverdure's slogan (p. 41). Or they repeat each other, as when Turandot mechanically reiterates what Charles has just said. At one point, Gabriel, Charles, Turandot and Trouscaillon have a long discussion over whether any of us can talk nonsense unless we have picked it up from someone else first. As the controversy lurches along, the word *connerie* acquires almost a plus-value, as it talking rubbish were something to admire (p. 71). There is a running comparison between the parrot and human beings. Gridoux, for one, maintains that parrots understand far more than is generally believed, and Madeleine adds: 'D'ailleurs nous, est-ce qu'on entrave vraiment kouak ce soit à kouak ce soit?' (p. 144). When the leering doorman at the queers' night-club asks the variegated crowd arriving with a parrot in a cage whether Laverdure is 'one of those' too, he goes on to complain that such creatures give him complexes. Gridoux at once suggests, excruciatingly, that the doorman consults a 'psittaco-analyst' (pp. 146-7). Laverdure's first change of tune is to speak suddenly in scholastic Latin: 'Nous ne comprenons pas le hic de ce nunc, ni le quid de ce quod' (p. 147), an instance of a reverse process of corruption, by which the parrot is infected by the human company he keeps. Later, during the brawl, struck in the perineum by a splinter of flying soup-tureen, Laverdure ends up silent at the bottom of his cage, traumatised. After the parrot is threatened with the stewpan by Aroun Arachide, his master Turandot, fearing for his own skin in the great stampede, comes up with the surrealistic proposal that he should get into the cage and let Laverdure carry him (p. 186).[20] Turandot's last words, before both 'take wing' along the Underground, are in fact the parrot's old refrain, whereas Laverdure himself cries 'Au revoir, les gars' (p. 187). Throughout, the parrot serves as a living reminder of the barminess of human language.

Now to the cataloguing. First of all, what I would call concertina-words (like the opening word of the novel, *Doukipudonktan?*) Queneau was always fascinated by the agglutinative tendency, the phonetic coagulation, of spoken French: that is, its habit of running words together into a continuous sound-pattern. This is clearly linked also with his interest in phonetic spelling. Furthermore, such reassembly of words ties in with the general theme, in this novel, of disguise. In fact, however, although such concertina-words puzzlingly seize the reader's attention, there are less than a score of them in the entire text.

Essméfie:	elle se méfie (p. 14)
Skeutadittaleur:	ce que tu as dit tout à l'heure (p. 10)
Cexé:	ce que c'est (p. 15)
Singermindépré:	Saint-Germain-des-Prés (p. 29)
Les coudocors:	les coudes au corps (p. 38)
Lagoçamilébou:	la gosse a mis les bouts (p. 37)
A boujpludutou:	elle ne bouge plus du tout (p. 47)

20 A similar threat (*passer à la casserole*) was earlier made by her father to Zazie, but the slang phrase there meant: 'you are going to be raped'.

Ltipstu:	le type se tut (p. 54)
Iadssa:	il y a de ça (p. 64)
Midineurs:	midi-dîneurs (p. 71)
Kouavouar:	quoi à voir (p. 91)
Vozouazévovos:	vos oies et vos veaux (p. 112)
Utu, upu, u:	eût eu (p. 126), eût pu, eût (p. 179)
Colochaussent:	collent aux chausses (p. 137)
A kimieumieu:	à qui mieux mieux (p. 167)
A stage-là:	à cet âge-là (p. 137)

Such contracted words accentuate the atmosphere of sudden spurts, surprise, frenzy (e.g. 'Immbondit dssus': 'il me bondit dessus' (p. 54) which gives great immediacy to the action of Zazie's father).

In addition, on the question of phonetic spelling, Queneau habitually writes *espliquer, egzactement*, and omits frequently the all but mute e (e.g. *ptite, je me ldemande*). Other phonetic spellings that might briefly throw the reader are *un kidan*: *un quidam* (p. 162) and *des ranbrans*: *des Rembrandt* (p. 146). Sometimes, in the goal of making strange, he twists the parts of a word about: *coca-cola—cacocalo* (p. 18). The fact that such comic devices are used so sparingly, so unsystematically, suggests that Queneau is suspicious of all systems, even his own, and that he recognises that to have written the whole novel along these lines would have produced something totally unreadable; the rhythm of reading would have been wrecked. As it is, the foreign reader has sometimes to stop in order to recite such peculiar forms aloud before the sou drops. In reflecting popular phonetic reality in these ways, Queneau is not being supercilious, not 'going slumming' condescendingly. Indeed, he was eager to quote, in *Bâtons, chiffres et lettres*, Proust's timely reminder about common linguistic origins: 'Les mots français que nous sommes si fiers de prononcer exactement ne sont eux-mêmes que des *cuirs* faits par des bouches gauloises, qui prononçaient de travers le latin et le saxon, notre langue n'étant que la prononciation défectueuse de quelques autres'.[21] Queneau's 'deliberate mistakes' have, in context, their own validity. As he said in *Bâtons, chiffres et lettres*: 'Il y a peu de fautes stériles' (p. 69).

---

[21] Proust, *Sodome et Gomorrhe*, Gallimard 1921-4, vol. IX, p. 176.

A variant on concertina-words are neologisms, coinages:

Factidiversialité:	the world of *fait-divers* (p. 36)
Euréquation:	cf. euréka! (p. 15)
Lessivophiles:	washday-lovers (p. 40)
Vuvurrer:	*susurrer voui* (p. 48)
Subtruquer:	to slip underneath (p. 101)
Un involontaire:	the opposite of a volunteer (p. 117)
Percontatif:	In English, 'percontation' (rare) is an enquiry which admits of a variety of answers, unlike 'interrogation' which admits only of yes or no.
Charluter:	Charles + *culbuter* (p. 145)
Une caromba:	mixture of the cancan and the rumba. And cf. the Spanish ¡*caramba*!
Mélancolieux:	*mélancolique* + *sérieux*
Somnivore:	sleep-destroying (p. 167)
Noctinaute:	night-traveller, cf. *cosmonaute* (p. 185)
Le vulgue homme Pécusse:	*vulgum pecus*, in Latin: the vile herd (p. 41)
L'orama:	a more limited panorama (p. 108)
Cicéroner:	cf. *cicérone*, a guide (p. 123)
Un fligolo:	*flic* + *gigolo* (p. 128)
Squeleptique:	*sceptique* + *squelettique* (p. 137)
Téléphonctionner:	the phone ringing (p. 137)
Rosir:	cf. *rougir* (p. 142)

All of these examples of neologisms reveal a writer eager to add to the existing stock of the French language, to fill in some of its gaps, some of the things it was previously unable to convey in quite so economical a way.

Much the same could be said of Queneau's anglicisms, or rather the English words which he gallicises in spelling (his contribution to *le franglais*):

Bicose (p. 22)
Linnecher: *lyncher* (p. 41)
Bloudjinnzes (p. 47)

Le baille-naïte:	Paris-By-Night tours, and a suggestion of yawning (p. 166)
Coboïlle:	cowboy (p 112)
Cornède bif (p. 134)	
Apibeursdé touillou:	'Happy Birthday to You' (p. 150)
Pimpons:	pingpong tables (p. 122)
Plède:	plaid (p. 119)
Claqueson (p. 93)	
Taximane (p. 101):	Also, *policemane* (p. 105), *flicmane* (p. 106)—all suggesting mania.

It seems to me that such gallicisations do not really make the foreign import look any more French or natural. They create in fact a new and intriguing monstrosity.[22]

Let us move on from lexicography to faults. Gabriel says, incorrectly, of Charles's taxi: 'Je nous le sommes réservé' (p. 13), and Veuve Mouaque: 'Faut peut-être pas mieux' (p. 111). In the main body of the narrative, Queneau himself at times uses deliberately mistaken forms: *oeils* (p. 84), 'Gabriel *fermit* les yeux', 'il se *tournit*', (p. 66), or *intervindre* (p. 131). He inserts several syntactical idiosyncrasies of popular French in the dialogue, e.g. the all-purpose and often superfluous *que* ('comment qu'il est venu?'). Perhaps these forms are meant to imply that the author himself has been contaminated by the corrupt speech of his characters, just as pronunciation affects spelling (*vise-à-vise* (p. 130)). He records incorrect liaisons: 'pour moi zossi' (p. 120), 'zarico verts' (p. 132).

I mentioned earlier Queneau's admiration for James Joyce's combination of various styles in *Ulysses*. Queneau's contribution in this field is to offer, for example, a medieval word-order: 'A l'étage second parvenue, sonne à la porte la neuve fiancée' (p. 140). Simple acts are often recounted in this mock-heroic way, and unlikely people spout the most elaborate kind of French. The imperfect subjunctive, for instance, has become largely comic to the French. Madeleine says to Gabriel: 'Vous n'avez jamais voulu que nous vous admirassions dans l'exercice de votre art' (p. 147). As

---

[22] From other languages: *Adspicez*: *adspice* (Latin) (p. 171), and *medza votche*: *mezza voce* (p. 66).

if envious of the greater manoeuvrability of English word-order, Queneau writes: 'Le rideau se magiquement divisa' (p. 148), and 'un vieil écorné carnet' (p. 112). Playing, on the other hand, with the possibilities for distinction by gender in French, he terms the queer waiter in a kilt *un Ecossaise* (p. 148). In the middle of supposedly trying to seduce Marceline, Bertin Poirée takes time off to worry about the correct form of the key verb *se vêtir*, which he mixes up with *s'en aller*: 'C'est français, ça, je me vêts? Je m'en vais, oui' (p. 161). He then says 'J'y vêts'. Mind you, after this puristic digression, Bertin Poirée brusquely reverts to the business in hand and orders Marceline to *se dévêtir*. From Dictionaries to sexual action, from one use of tongues to another.[23]

Dictionaries lead on to lists. Mathematics, besides, gave Queneau the ambition of exhaustive enumeration. Often such an urge leads to the inflation of the minimal ('De superbes gratte-ciel à quatre ou cinq étages' (p. 44)), though the gentle Marceline has a refrain: 'N'exagérons rien' (p. 142). On several occasions, Queneau exploits lists, perhaps as a way of illustrating the runaway potentialities of language; the way words can take over and generate their own momentum. Trouscaillon dressed as a *flic* menaces Gabriel with this list of possible charges: poncing, fleecing, 'hormosexuality', eonism and congenital malformation of the male *glans* (p. 66). Where is the joke here? Like Rabelais centuries before, Queneau simultaneously shows off, and belittles his own recondite knowledge, and thereby creates comedy out of weird conglomerations of words. In that speech on the café-terrace, Gabriel wavers between a Shakespearian lament, pinched from *Hamlet*, on 'the slings and arrows of outrageous fortune', and this inventory: the price of groceries, the smell of cauliflower, and the passivity of wooden horses (p. 117). Again, with the aim of concocting a comic pell-mell, Queneau details the goods available in the grocer's and a chemist's, alternately: camomile, *pâté de campagne*, caramel, santonica,[24] gruyère cheese and cupping glasses (p. 126). Parodying the typical French policeman's demand to see 'vos papiers', Trouscaillon demands: an identity-card, Social Security number, an

---

23 Cf. *Les Fleurs bleues*, p. 48: *la languistique*.
24 A wormwood derivative used against intestinal worms.

electricity-bill, and a Papal Bull (p. 164). Another variety of the list
occurs with crops of synonyms, as when Zazie asks: 'Qu'est-ce que
c'est au juste qu'une tante? Une pédale? une lope? un pédé? un
hormosessuel? Y a des nuances?' (p. 129). Haven't we all felt something akin to this when consulting a foreign dictionary? Lastly, the
catalogue of identical offences which the two cycle-cops deafeningly
accuse the riotous gang with Gabriel of committing: 'Chahut lunaire,
boucan somnivore, médianoche gueulante' (p. 171).

In the general area of wordplay, and though they overlap often
with neologisms, puns hold a place apart. In *Petite cosmogonie
portative*, Queneau clearly assigned to the pun a primordial function:
'De quelque calembour naît signification' (p. 129), and in *Oeuvres
complètes de Sally Mara*, he expressed the urge to 'élever le calembour à la hauteur d'un supplice' (p. 349).[25] And that is precisely
what he does in *Zazie dans le métro* with this concatenation of
geometrical and rhetorical puns: ' "Ça, faut avouer", dit Trouscaillon
qui dans cette simple ellipse, utilisait hyperboliquement le cercle
vicieux de la parabole' (p. 115). Gabriel says: 'C'est tout de même
embêtant de se mettre à dos un bourin' (p. 66), with its unwilling
double-entendre: the possibly queer Gabriel talking of getting on
the wrong side of a policeman. When he throws Trouscaillon down-
stairs, we see the pun on *vider les ordures*: (a) to put the household
rubbish out, (b) to kick nuisances off the premises. After he has
been thrown in a heap, Trouscaillon asks the barman for a pick-me-
up (p. 67). When the guide Gabriel has apparently been abducted,
Veuve Mouaque cries out: 'Aux guidenappeurs!' (p. 104). Sometimes the verbal sport takes the form of playing on similar sounds,
as when, in his soliloquy on the ephemeral nature of life, Gabriel
laments: 'Un rien l'amène, un rien l'anime, un rien la mine, un rien
l'emmène' (p. 117). The puns are often pointed (and, etymologically,
'pun' may derive from the Italian *punto*). When Zazie, obsessed
with the double meaning of *tante*, asks her perennial question:
'C'est un hormo?', Fédor Balanovitch answers smartly: 'Tu veux
dire un normal' (p. 122). This is a grammatical correction, for it
sounds as if Zazie has used a plural form of the noun with a singular
article, and a kind of oneupmanship, by which Fédor asserts his own
sexual orthodoxy, his 'straightness'. Gabriel denies that his act has

[25] *Les Fleurs bleues* even has a talking horse fond of puns (see p. 11).

anything to do with vulgar *slip-tize* (p. 151). When he performs his routine, the tourists shout encouragingly: 'Go, femme' (p. 152). If they had shouted 'Go, homme', he might have departed there in high dudgeon. A sideboard typifying bourgeois bad taste and known properly as *le genre Henri II* becomes 'le buffet genre hideux' (p. 156).

Sometimes, however, the punning is pointless, gratuitous, as in Madeleine's mixing of fashion jargon and estate-agent's abbreviations: 'Un tailleur deux pièces salle de bains avec un chemisier porte-jarretelles cuisine' (p. 142). 'Libre comme l'r' (p. 110), 'tabac . . . passage à tabac' (p. 170), *encre* (*ancre*) (p. 34), *cercueil . . . bière* (p. 21) are other examples, fit only for the 'Almanach Vermot'. There are two *contre-pèteries*, or Spoonerisms: *muscadine/grenadet* (p. 185), and *friser l'injure/frisure* (p. 172).

Puns are one kind of overlaying: the fusion of two words or concepts. Another kind is allusion: cultural, historical, social or linguistic, usually twisted in some fashion.

(1) 'Il flairait la paille dans les poutrelles . . .' (p. 13): cf. the Bible: 'Voir la paille dans l'oeil de son voisin et ne pas voir la poutre dans le sien' (to see the mote in one's brother's eye). cf. also various songs of Georges Brassens where women fluctuate between being *vaches* and *poupées*, e.g. 'Une jolie fleur dans une peau de vache'.

(2) 'Les prouesses des trois orfèvres' (p. 26): This is a ribald song in which three goldsmiths visit a bourgeois home, eat and drink copiously and, not content with that, 'ils baisent le père au cul, la mère au con', and then go to the roof to 'baiser le chat'.[26]

(3) 'Les visiteurs du soir' (p. 30): An allusion to Marcel Carné's film of that name.

(4) 'Ballons Lamoricière (p. 44): i.e. the producer Albert Lamorisse and his films *Le Voyage en ballon* or *Le Ballon rouge*.

(5) 'Forain talon-rouge' (p. 48): A twist on a phrase by Raymond Roussel, *le forban talon-rouge*. Louis XIV's male courtiers wore shoes with red heels.

---

[26] See: 'Le chat lui-même y aurait passé' (p. 53).

(6) 'Les voies du silence' (p. 93): cf. André Malraux's art-study, *Les Voix du silence*.

(7) 'L'heure où les gardiens de musée vont boire' (p. 99): cf. Victor Hugo, 'Booz endormi': 'C'était l'heure tranquille où les lions vont boire'.

(8) 'Gibraltar aux anciens parapets' (p. 99). cf. Arthur Rimbaud's 'Bateau ivre': 'Je regrette l'Europe aux anciens parapets'.

(9) 'Garçons vêtus d'un pagne . . . démis de bière enrhumés' (p. 130): cf. Guillaume Apollinaire: 'La Chanson du Mal-Aimé': 'Les cafés gonflés de fumée / crient tout l'amour de leurs tziganes / De tous leurs siphons enrhumés / De leurs garçons vêtus d'un pagne'.

(10) 'Intermittences de son coeur bon' (p. 130): cf. Proust's theory of sporadic love, 'les intermittences du coeur'.

(11) 'Voyez mes ailes' (p. 171): French cycle-policemen are often called *hirondelles de nuit* because of their capes. And cf. La Fontaine: 'La Chauve-souris et les deux belettes': 'Grâce à l'Auteur de l'Univers, / Je suis oiseau, voyez mes ailes'. This is a poem in praise of quick thinking and chameleonic personalities (cf. Trouscaillon).

(12) 'La soupe à l'oignon qui berce' (p. 174): cf. Baudelaire's poems on consolatory wine.

(13) 'Chars nocturnes' (p. 179): Here Queneau plays triple games. *Char nocturne* was already a Romantic circumlocution for the moon. Queneau returns it to its original (and now archaic) sense of 'night-vehicles'.

(14) 'St'urbe inclite qu'on vocite Parouart' (p. 121): this famous city we call Paris. In Rabelais's *Pantagruel*, the scholar from Limoges gallicises Latin in this way: 'De la célèbre académie que l'on vocite Lutèce'.

(15) 'Mont-de-piété' (p. 120): In slang, a pawnshop, also called *chez ma tante*. *Tante* is slang for homosexual. An appropriate name, therefore, for this specialised nightclub.

(16) 'Ambre lunaire' (p. 70): cf. 'Ambre solaire', suntan lotion.

(17) 'Musc argenté' (p. 70): *Renard argenté* is a more expensive

kind of fur, so, by analogy, this is a dearer version of simple musk.

(18) 'Etoile-Rouge de Neuflize' (p. 53): Neuflize is the name of a banking family, unlikely therefore to support any 'Red Star' team.

(19) 'Montjoie Sainte-Chapelle!' (p. 104): cf. the rallying-cry of the Kings of France: 'Montjoie Saint-Denis!'

(20) 'La terre verte' (p. 148): cf. the parrot's name, Laverdure. *La terre jaune* is a slang term for homosexual terrain.

(21) 'Eau d'arquebuse' (p. 68): usually, *eau d'arquebusade*, an infusion or lotion made from plants and a once popular remedy. This variant makes it sound like a weapon, hence the follow-up about *l'eau atomique*.

(22) 'Jitrouas' (p. 57): 'J3', an age-category for rationing purposes during the Occupation. Later, any cocky urchin.

(23) 'Eonisme' (p. 66): For the Gnostics, the 'eons' were emanations of the Deity and eternal likewise. The Chevalier d'Eon, a French secret agent (1728-1810) was best known for his transvestism. Thus *eonism* suggests the two aspects of Gabriel: angelism and sexual ambiguity.

(24) 'Transtrucs en commachin' (p. 94): *transports en commun. Truc* and *machin* are often used to fill in for the proper term.

(25) 'Faut de tout pour faire une guerre' (p. 49): Usually, '. . . *un monde'.*

(26) 'Laver son linge sale en famille' (p. 40): A literalising twist on the adage about washing one's dirty linen in private.

(27) 'Liquette ninque' (p. 40): *Le hic et nunc* (with French pronunciation), the present moment. In slang, *liquette* = shirt.

(28) 'Le zest de la situation' (p. 105): Usually only used in *entre le zist et le zest*. Here *le zest* therefore suggests some dubious element.

What is the point of so many allusions? Is it a matter of the in-joke, of incestuous culture? No doubt this is partly so, but, more modestly, Queneau is clearly ready to enrich his own text by prestigious imports, and, at the same time, to guy these monuments of culture, as he twists the French language itself.

A further aspect of the language-game is the sport with foreign languages, which Zazie calls, in an Italianism (*forestiere*) 'les langues forestières' (p. 92). Gridoux suddenly comes out with a Latin tag: 'Ne sutor ultra crepidam' (the shoemaker should stick to his last). And, when he utters the mishmash 'Usque non ascendam, anch'io son pittore, adios amigos', he appears to think that these are all Latin sayings (p. 78).[27] The point Queneau is making here is surely that all our heads are ragbags of miscellaneous junk, but that from this chaos we can salvage grains of sense. As well as the unlikeliness of people like Gridoux spouting foreign languages, Queneau reverses the coin, and has his tourists speaking archaic French picked up from Berlitz schools.[28] When, to everybody's surprise, Gabriel utters a few consecutive words in English, he makes out that some sort of miracle has happened, that he has been granted the gift of tongues (p. 123). On the basis of the word *xénophobie*, Queneau coins the noun *xénophones*: speakers of foreign languages. In a sense, for him, we all speak our native tongue as if it were a foreign language. It is, or should be, a source of perpetual astonishment to us. In a way, it speaks us as much as we speak it.

Zazie dans le métro features a great deal of what can variously be called slang, popular speech or the vernacular. Much of this slang is essentially Parisian and lower-class, but not, I think proletarian. Slang can be a rich sub-language, as it often appears here, wheareas proletarian speech is surely impoverished. The desire to mock nobility, to debag poshness, to puncture pretentiousness, must be a major element in the use of slang, although, of course, its deliberate use merely replaces one kind of rhetoric with another in a lower key. Lower? Queneau is obviously trying to ennoble slang as much as to belittle elevated language. Throughout this novel, therefore, he alternates, and often mixes together, the lofty and the low. This had led one critic of Queneau, Daubercies, to claim that Queneau's readers need to be 'bi-lingual' (*6*, p. 81). As well

---

[27] There is a link between the two quotations, for the first was said by Apellus the painter to a cobbler who fancied himself as an art-critic. 'Anch'io son pittore' was the title Apollinaire once thought of for his *Calligrammes*.

[28] Cf. the camper in *Les Fleurs bleues* who speaks 'European' (p. 15).

as insults, obscenities and French strewn with popular errors, all of the characters can, on occasion, emit a mouthful like this statement of Gridoux's to Gabriel: 'Vous qui jetiez le voile pudique de l'ostracisme sur la circonscription de vos activités', which is a misuse of words, anyway (p. 147). Or this description: 'Gabriel extirpa de sa manche une pochette de soie mauve et s'en tamponna le tarin', where the conjunction of elegance and the vernacular still preserves for the gesture a certain stylishness (p. 9). Queneau in fact plays the two styles off against each other, so that each scores points against the opponent but neither wins outright. In calling mussels by their technical name *lamellibranches* (p. 50), by using words like *pseudopodes* (p. 69) to describe liquid spreading on a table, *vulcanisante* (p. 107) to suggest amorous heat, or *lampadophore* (p. 186) for Marceline holding an electric torch, Queneau reveals his love of pedantry as much as of slang. Likewise, he often narrates simple acts in heroic style. Sometimes, he resorts to circumlocution, as when a husband is referred to longwindedly as 'celui qu'avait le droit de la grimper légalement' (p. 10), or when Trouscaillon's lust is described in this strange but telling way: 'Il aurait eu tendance à attendrir le cuir de son comportement dans le sperme de ses desiderata' (p. 163). All in all, with this variety of styles, it is obvious that Queneau never tries seriously to offer a tape-recording of spoken French. He states unambiguously in *Bâtons, chiffres et lettres* that the writer interested in such matters has to *stylise* the oral language he uses (p. 191). This is because it is impossible to capture and to reproduce exactly the spoken via the written without freezing it to death. All that can be achieved is a suggestive approximation. Queneau himself has always refused to draw any evaluative distinction between popular and literary French. He uses both with equal naturalness. Thereby, he makes a splendid virtue out of necessity (for we do not speak like books), and a silk purse from a sow's ear.

8 Grand finale and con-clusion

Zazie dans le métro was Queneau's biggest success in the field of fiction. It represents about half (500,000 copies) of the total sales of his work. A year after its appearance, Louis Malle's splendid film of the book, vigorously exploiting the techniques of silent comedies, amplified this success. What struck most reviewers, and presumably many readers, of the novel was, unsurprisingly, the scandalously foul language of young Zazie herself, as well as her Lolita-type sexual adventures. Many, too, relished the anarchic upheaval of accepted values provoked by this *enfant terrible*, and the general wave of uncertainty introduced into several dimensions of the adult world by her presence. Queneau's experiments with combining diametrically opposed stylistic registers encouraged some critics, fatally in general, to ape his technique of concertina-words. On the other hand, some of the snootier men of letters jibbed at the popular acclaim, and argued that this novel, far from being a creation of great verve and freshness, represented in fact the worn-out sport of a blasé mandarin, toying with the slummier aspects of existence. Altogether, however, the response was overwhelmingly praising, and some more honest critics had the grace to admit that, most probably, there was much more to this novel than at first met the lazy eye.

Nabokov said of his novel *Lolita* that it was not primarily centred on the sexual liaison of an ageing man and a nymphet, but that it more importantly celebrated the love affair of a Russian émigré with the English language.[29] This was clearly true in some sense, but novels do, after all, contain *people* of some kind or another. And so, although I hold to my view that *Zazie dans le métro* is principally concerned with the phenomenon of language, in the end we have to come back to its human denizens, for the grand finale. For that is truly what it is. The concluding section of the

[29] Nabokov, *Lolita*, London: Corgi, 1961, p. 334.

novel grows increasingly violent. Vast mobs of police suddenly materialise to besiege the hero and his friends, as in a Keystone Cops silent comedy. In addition, there are two armoured divisions of nightwatchmen and a squadron of camel-troops originating improbably from the Jura mountains in eastern France (p. 182). It is a kind of surrealist holocaust, an accelerating smash-up. We witness too a mad proliferation of waiters, who assail the gigantic Gabriel. Alliteratively, he knocks their heads together, 'de telle force et belle façon que les deux farauds s'effondrent fondus' (p. 178). An epic combat ensues, in which the said waiters are flung off him like water off the proverbial duck's back, or raindrops from the rear wheels of a juggernaut lorry. (These are my similes. Queneau's writing is catching. When you read him, you want to write or speak like him.) Queneau himself puts it this way: 'Like a giant beetle attacked by a column of warrior-ants, like an ox assailed by leeches' (p. 179). The description is clearly mock-heroic: Queneau is playing a pastiche variation on the epic military encounters of his favourite author, Homer ('O père de toute littérature et de tout scepticisme', as Queneau exclaimed in *Bâtons, chiffres et lettres* (p. 124)). As well as the brawls, there is knockabout farce, when Gabriel and company, to celebrate their victory, try to make themselves a *café-crème* on an unfamiliar machine and scald various parts of their anatomy in the process (p. 181).

There is sudden death. Veuve Mouaque is mowed down. Her last, poignant words are: 'C'est bête. Moi qu'avais des rentes' (p. 184). It is difficult to be sure how to take this sudden intrusion of death into the farcical battle. Is it black comedy, a reminder that serious, fatal things *also* happen to people, or what? After the often zany but potentially everyday events of the preceding parts, the fantasy ending may well leave some readers unsatisfied and bewildered. In the film-version, the official besiegers were given extremely sinister military accoutrements, and there was a strong suggestion that the mad little world of the heroes was being threatened by the apparatus of a police-state. But this inter-pretation by the director might merely reflect the time at which the film was made, a period of civil violence in France as the Algerian War dragged to its bloody conclusion. Politics figures to some degree in several of Queneau's novels, e.g. the rise of fascist parties in the 1930s in *Les Enfants du limon*, but is totally absent from *Zazie dans le métro*. From the viewpoint of connexions with *l'histoire universelle*, it is probably, like *Saint-Glinglin*, his most timeless book.

Though she and Veuve Mouaque land some timely blows before they respectively faint and die, Zazie is spared some of the final horrors by periodically falling asleep. Gabriel's speech at the Eiffel Tower had already introduced the possibility of life being a dream, and it has been suggested that the whole story is possibly a child's reverie. The name of the café where the finale takes place lends some support to this view. It is called 'Aux Nyctalopes'. Nyctalopia is that peculiarity of vision called day-blindness, and it refers to those people who see better in the dark than in daylight, as dreamers do. On the other hand, the ultimate carnage might indicate that, not knowing how else to wrap up his story, Queneau opted for a violent and startling climax. For, as well as striving to keep a kind of mathematical control over his plots, Queneau was always conscious of the arbitrary nature of all fictional creation. For example, at the end of *Pierrot mon ami*, he speculates on 'le roman que cela aurait pu faire' (p. 210). Gabriel and his friends are rescued from the encircling forces of so-called order (for the police in this novel beget chaos) by the old pantomime device of the *deux ex machina*—in this instance they all sink out of sight and harm's way on a serving-hoist, operated from the basement by Marceline, whence they make good their escape via the sewers into a Métro tunnel. Zazie's ambition is at last fulfilled; ironically, she is not conscious of the fact.

When Zazie's mother concludes her dirty weekend in Paris, she hurries to the station where the story began, still feigning to be concerned about her daughter. But Zazie's only response to the question: 'What did you do?' is the ambiguous phrase: 'J'ai vieilli'. This can mean either: 'I've grown old', or 'I've grown older'. It could be a deliberate anti-climax, or it might imply that, in growing older over the weekend, Zazie has learnt something from the experience. When, however, we recall the representatives of the older generation in this novel, it seems improbable that age brings any improvement in wisdom. Perhaps we should settle for taking her words as a simple state of fact. Throughout the novel, indeed, Zazie has operated as an insistent fact, in contrast with the looniness, dreaminess and evasiveness of the adults.

The view, mentioned earlier, that Queneau's fictional world could be seen as largely ritual in essence is emphasised by Brée and Guiton, who talk in their chapter on Queneau, of 'the impression of dance, stately or orgiastic, but always ceremonial in nature'. They go on to argue that most activity in his universe is impractical: 'Assiduous attendance at the movies, walks devoid of destination, conversations often devoid of meaning, quests devoid of object'. They stress the significance of the title of one novel, *Le Dimanche de la vie*—the day *par excellence* for ritualised non-work (*19*, p. 173). That novel's epigraph from Hegel, remarking on the joviality of many Dutch paintings, runs: 'It is the Sunday of Life, which brings all to one level and removes all badness, simply as such. Men who are thus so whole-heartedly of good temper can neither be wholly bad nor mean'. Allowance made for the national sport of cheerful insult, much the same could be said of *Zazie dans le métro*. The fixed routine of Gridoux's lunch, of Gabriel's self-manicure, the time-honoured imprecations, the congealed pontificating, Charles's passive acquiescence to conventional marriage; no wonder that Queneau uses the word *inoccupations* to describe how his people use their time (p. 33). They are *flâneurs*, like Cidrolin in *Les Fleurs bleues* who is characterised by a 'manque de comportement' (p. 46). Marginal people in marginal activities. Though they race about Paris a great deal, the heroes of *Zazie dans le métro* are not looking for anything in particular. They have it already: a mode of existence, which nothing substantially alters; they are what they are. This most mobile of all Queneau's novels is also his most essentially static.

Queneau expressed his admiration for Louis Malle's film of the book, but stressed that novels and films are really two very different things. This is especially true in the case of a novel like *Zazie dans le métro*, where so much revolves around language, never the strong point of the silver screen. Certainly, some of the incidental jokes in this novel could hardly be translated into cinematic images. For example: 'Elles entendaient, au loin, dans les rues, les pneus se dégonfler dans la nuit' (p. 143). Marceline and Madeleine also hear the moonlight grilling on a T.V. aerial. These notations record something physically impossible; it is purely in the mind, imagined.

Or the scene when a man, who stops his car in heavy traffic, suddenly starts off again, as if propelled by the gusts of air emanating from
the angry hooters of the vehicles behind (p. 114). Or finally, the nice
observation that, if you are sitting in a basement café, all you can see
outside, if you are lucky, is people's feet, or perhaps an entire dog,
provided that it is a basset-hound (p. 21). On the other hand, and
here the screen version excels, crowd-scenes in cafés, in the streets,
at the flea-market or the Eiffel Tower, can be even more successfully captured on film.[30] Within the novel itself, there are several
references to the cinema. While everyone else in the flat is asleep,
Zazie makes a reconnoitre of it before making her escape, concocting as she does so a variant on a fairy-tale (*Sleeping Beauty*).
But she bores herself with her own inventions and soon prefers the
living cinema of the streets outside to the pictures on her inner
screen (p. 132). On the other hand, when Turandot has narrowly
evaded being lynched by the mob of outraged bystanders, he plays
over his fright on his mental T.V. screen once back in the safety of
his bar (p. 36). Queneau frequently stresses the spill-over of cinema
into everyday life (e.g. 'le type sourit diaboliquement, comme au
cinéma' (p. 62)). The word *cinéma* is used by Zazie, depending
on her mood, both praisingly and pejoratively. She ridicules Veuve
Mouaque's infatuation with Trouscaillon by saying dismissively:
'Tout ça, c'est du cinéma' (p. 127), whereas, as we saw earlier,
in her account of her would-be rapist father, the cinema then represents for her the height of excitement: when he mimics a screen
villain, she enjoys the spectacle enormously.

I have mentioned silent-film comedies. Like them, the narrative
of *Zazie dans le métro* is very jumpy, staccato. The graphic present
is used frequently, often in the same sentence as the past historic,
and such *temps mêlés* promote great immediacy. There are many
brusque changes of pace. There are numerous sudden digressions,
when any of the characters can be easily distracted from the matter
in hand by expatiating arguments about ethics, geography, language
or citizen's rights. Thus, as well as frenetic action, there is much
stalling, or time wasting (see pp. 42-3). There are swift changes of

---

30 *Zazie dans le métro* has also been adapted for the stage, and there is a
strip-cartoon version of it; a form of popular culture which, together
with science-fiction, Queneau always relished.

scene, the details of which are sometimes omitted, and these tie in with the repeated theme of quick-change metamorphoses (p. 37). I have several times stressed how fascinated Queneau was by shapes and structures. He gives us many repetitions, slogans, refrains, convinced, as he says in *Les Fleurs bleues*, that 'la répétition est l'une des plus odiférantes fleurs de la rhétorique' (p. 65). One such motto can be found in any guide-book: 'La Sainte-Chapelle, joyau de l'art gothique' (93). Two separate motorists repeat to Trouscaillon almost word for word the same bellyaching speech. Another variant pattern is that of the reversal or criss-cross (as when Gabriel talks of his 'infériorité de complexe' (p. 42)). After Zazie eludes Turandot by publicly accusing him of wanting to molest her, she tries to pull off the same ploy with Trouscaillon, only to find that he beats her to it by accusing her of stealing his parcel of blue-jeans (p. 57). This is what Queneau meant by that 'rhyming' of situations mentioned earlier. Similarly, his impatience with verbal linearity, with the fact that words, unlike fugal music, cannot cause several things to synchronise, makes him attempt briefly simultaneity, as when Gabriel and Veuve Mouaque speak at the same time: 'Qu'est-ce que / (Oh qu'il est mignon) / t'insinues / (il m'a appelée) / sur mon compte / (une mousmé)' (p. 170). And, at every turn, we see coincidence of meetings; Paris is here seen in the light of the cliché as *un grand village*, where everyone lives in each other's pockets. In *Le Vol d'Icare*, we get a reversed Pirandello situation, in which four authors go in search of their characters who have escaped from their manuscripts. Queneau goes on to speculate that, one day, novels, while still surviving as an art-form, will no longer have characters (p. 74). It is reminiscent of Flaubert's unrealisable dream of a book about nothing, held together by internal force of style.

A French critic, Paul Gayot, said of *Le Chiendent* something that could relevantly be applied to *Zazie dans le métro*: that the apparent randomness of the plot is equalled only by its rigorous shape; that the game has its rules, which are infringed only at the very end, where the adventure topples over into fantasy, and the chess-match turns into a skittle-tournament (*9*, p. 75). Queneau's world, in this novel as elsewhere, is one of controlled anarchy, if not here, as in other of his fictions, one of mathematical games with structure. Today, when critics, in France especially, grow increasingly ludic, it is refreshing to encounter a creator, a first-hand practitioner, adopting the game approach. The great Dutch cultural historian, Huizinga, in his study of the play-element in human society, repeatedly makes the point that the essence of play is rules, clear frameworks governing the action. (It is notorious, too, that theatrical farces rely on the creation of a highly structured chaos.) 'You can deny', states Huizinga, 'if you like, nearly all abstractions: justice, beauty, truth, goodness, mind, God. You can deny seriousness, but not play'.[31] What is indisputable, moreover, is Queneau's own palpable enjoyment in writing this effervescent work. He told Marguerite Duras that, here, he felt he was doing exactly what and as he wanted, without worrying about the need to renew himself or to be especially serious (*22*, p. 27).

But even comic, playful novels make their points. Roland Barthes argues that *Zazie dans le métro* is governed by negativity, by *dérision* or duplicity, the ingredients of which he lists in this way (*15*, p. 676). Firstly, the title is an *antiphrase*, a contradiction in terms, as Zazie nevers uses the Métro (at least, in a conscious state). There is constant uncertainty (e.g. about the correct names of public buildings). There is the coexistence of contrary roles (Trouscaillon is both *un satyre* and *un flic*). There is much confusion about sexuality. There is 'tautology' (one policeman is arrested by another). There is reversal or upheaval (a child brutalising an adult). The style is largely a parody of other styles. Now, all this is true, but I am not persuaded that it adds up to anything so ponderous as *dérision* (total mockery of all things). I think Queneau's approach is nuanced. For example, the words *impartial* or *objectif* crop up quite often, yet in general his people are entirely subjective. They see their own little corners of the world and little else. *L'histoire universelle* has little hold over them, except insofar as it excites their mirth (p. 68). When Gabriel makes his grandiloquent gestures and statements (e.g. 'la vérité, comme si tu savais cexé. Comme si quelqu'un au monde savait cexé. Tout ça (geste), tout ça c'est du bidon; le Panthéon, les Invalides, oui du bidon' (p. 17)), he is amusing, but you cannot really wipe out such solid edifices with just words. And, of course, it could be ignorance, rather than the impossibility of knowing anything for sure, which is being demonstrated here.

[31] J. Huizinga, *Homo Ludens*, London: Paladin, 1970, p. 2.

What is more, much of the time Gabriel lives richly enough in the real here-and-now, *le hic et nunc* ('liquette ninque, celle qu'il n'est pas si facile de laver' (p. 40)). Reality cannot entirely be washed, or wished, away. 'Accepter la réalité', Queneau wrote in *Voyage en Grèce*, 'c'est l'accepter dans sa totalité, le plaisir comme la douleur, le bien comme le mal, le jour comme la nuit, l'été comme l'hiver' (p. 172).

All the same, there is much room for doubt (Queneau has the courage of his dubieties). Of Gridoux struggling to think, Queneau writes tentatively: 'On pourrait presque dire qu'il semblerait qu'il a l'air de réfléchir à quelque chose' (pp. 76-7). In great exasperation at one point, Trouscaillon complains that words no longer mean what they used to mean (p. 105). But on the other hand, this novel is marked not only by instability (cf. the sudden disappearances denoted by the verbs *se barrer, s'éclipser, mettre les bouts, filer*), but also by perseverance (the parrot, Zazie). I believe the epigraph from Aristotle gives us a clue to Queneau's intentions.[32] 'Ho plasas ephanisen': 'The poet fabricated and abolished it'. The reference is to a certain wall in Homer's poem, and Aristotle is expressing his doubt whether such a wall ever existed in fact, or whether it was merely a poet's fabrication which, being made of words, can also be verbally abolished (unlike the Panthéon). Queneau is here hinting that he is exercising the novelist's right to create a world and then finally to smash it to pieces, as in the epic brawl in the café, rather like the auto-destruct objects of some modern sculptors, by what he spells as *un queneau-coutte* (*un knockout*) in *Les Derniers Jours* (p. 65). But the building-up is as important to him as the knocking-down. He cannot be seen, as he is by Barthes, as principally a negator. Aristotle's statement is a dialectical proposition (cf. Queneau's admiration for the great dialectician, Hegel). If so, where is the synthesis, which in the Hegelian dialectic, should follow the thesis and antithesis? Typically, Queneau wriggles away at this juncture. We could translate the Aristotle quotation by 'now you see it, now you don't'—the archetypal patter of the prestidigitator (of which there is at least one powerful embodiment in *Le Chiendent*). Indeed, Queneau has always been entranced by this art of magical

---

[32] Strabo quotes these words of Aristotle in his *Geography*, vol IX, London: Heinemann, 1929, p. 71.

production and disappearance. According to *Bords,* one of the projected volumes of the 'Encyclopédie de la Pléiade' would have for theme: 'L'Illusion, l'Erreur et le Mensonge, scientifiquement traités à partir de la prestidigitation et de la sophistique (invention grecque laquelle, comme on le sait, avait pour but de faire passer le vrai pour faux et le faux pour vrai)' (p. 108). Queneau is one such *sophisticated* writer. In *Le Chiendent,* he exploits the Surrealist coinage *littératurer* (*littérature + raturer*): creation is self-effacing.

The artist is free, specially so, within his own rules, but the reader of Queneau, too, is invited to exercise freedom. The running joke about *(geste)*—gestures which are never specified—implies firstly that other writers commonly go in for elaborate descriptions of characters' gestures, as a roundabout way of conveying their emotional or mental states. This habit strikes Queneau as something of a con, for in ordinary life human gesticulations do not invariably communicate anything very precise. Literature thus often makes people out to be more readable, more intelligible, than they actually are. Furthermore, this joke offers a kind of do-it-yourself to the reader. We can fill in the details of the gesture for ourselves, very easily sometimes, as when *le flic* gestures to suggest where *he* would stuff priests (p. 172). There is a similar joke about *(détail)* and *(silence)* or even *(silence double)*. For as well as the gap between written and spoken French, Queneau is interested in that between spoken and what he calls *oral* French: i.e. language considered in its total environment of gestures, grunts, coughs, etc. (see *Bâtons, chiffres et lettres*, p. 87). Amidst all the laughter at human lunacy, some of the madness has its own special charm, as in the delirious, circuitous logic of Gridoux's lunchtime eating-arrangements. He eats on the spot, so as not to miss out on any customers, but, as none ever comes at that hour, he can eat in peace. This is described as a double advantage (p. 73). Much of the comedy in *Zazie dans le métro* does not really set out to destroy language as in the early plays of Ionesco, for Queneau constantly recognises that much fun is to be had from pitting words against each other. For instance, as cybernetics is the science of mechanical communication, when Charles speaks on the telephone, he utters 'le mot cybernétique: "Allô" ' (p. 137). The French tongue *is* looking peaky; it needs all the tonics it can get. As Queneau commented in *Bâtons, chiffres et lettres*, if he is operating on a dying language, it is in order to save the child alive and kicking in its womb and, in so doing, to save the mother as well; a Caesarian operation (p. 25).

This novel centres on contagion, it is a verbal epidemic. The slang word *illico* corrupts the nearby Anglicism *bicose* to form *bellicose* (p. 125). Zazie affects everyone. Cinema and everyday life overlap. ('L'Uni-Park', in *Pierrot mon ami*, is both the real 'Luna-Park' in Paris and, as with the American 'Beat' poet Ferlinghetti, a 'Coney Island of the mind'.) It was in relation to that novel that Camus spoke of Queneau's 'matter-of-fact fantasy' (*20*, p. 1929). Indeed, Queneau's people often adopt the tactic of *nil admirari*; the stall-holder is 'pas déconcerté' by Trouscaillon's aggressive behaviour (p. 49). In *Zazie dans le métro*, we are treated to a mutual contamination of the real and the unreal, so that everyday occurrences are fantasised, just as Zazie herself proceeds from waking experiences to dream. It is easy to pigeonhole Queneau's people as puppets, but surely they retain considerable vestiges of normal recognisable humanity. After all, most of us, at some moments, behave like caricatures of human beings. Do not forget that the amorous widow is called 'Madame Mouaque. Comme tout le monde' (p. 107). It is true that Queneau blows all kinds of raspberries at various allegedly hallowed institutions: the French language, conventional respectability, human reason. But think of children's rudeness, which is often a mixture of aggressiveness and affection. Queneau is tangibly fond of what he mocks, and he never leaves himself out of the firing line. As Claude Roy said, there is a certain perverseness in Queneau which leads him to use his intelligence to express stupidity, his curiosity to translate boredom, and his inventivenesss to feature platitudes (*29*, p. 83).

It may well be that, on the deepest level, Queneau believed that, apart from in the special world of mathematics, the only realm any of us is really capable of inhabiting is that of platitude. Perhaps the *commonplace* (and his idol Flaubert certainly subscribed to this sombre view) is where we all live. It was this kind of bleak possibility in Queneau's work which incited the distinguished French thinker, Gaston Bachelard, to say: 'Queneau, c'est de la dynamite, déguisée en barbe à papa' (see *5*, p. 336). The *éminence grise* of modern French literature, Jean Paulhan, studied the 'Hain-

Tenys' of Madagascar, unanswerable traditional proverbs used in arguments as a form of aggressive self-defence. We hear muted echoes of this strategy in *Zazie dans le métro*, where so much agonistic arguing goes on. In *Le Chiendent*, a character 'constate avec amertume que ces banalités correspondent parfaitement à la réalité' (p. 16). And as Flaubert and Sartre also discovered, a fascination with banality can occasion vertigo in the observer.[33] Perhaps it is to counter such dangers that the hero of *Pierrot mon ami* 'thinks of nothing a great deal' (p. 200)—and here 'nothing' is granted the strange positive quality given it in *Alice* by that other great literary mathematician, Lewis Carroll.[34] The truest statement Queneau makes in his entire corpus comes in *Pierrot mon ami*: 'Du temps eut lieu' (p. 82).

Wherever he is now, and if he is in a position to observe our attempts to analyse and evaluate his work, Queneau would no doubt be quaking with merriment at the folly of the enterprise. Yet at the same time he would accept that this is what people in fact get up to: reading each other. His mockery never completely undermines his basic tolerance. But he was by temperament elusive, escaping the net of words and ideas that others tried to snare him with. He was a great frustrater or reverser of expectations. The Métro is on strike till the last page of the novel featuring it in its title; in *Le Chiendent* various characters hunt for a treasure which exists only in their own imaginations; *Pierrot mon ami* is a detective-story with no real enigma and no tying-up of loose ends. Queneau's people rarely make any noticeable progress, and indeed often regress. Above all, the reader is frequently reminded, honestly, that he is reading a book, an artificial construct ('Pourquoi "cette fois-ci"? demanda Marceline, en roulant les derniers mots de sa question entre des guillemets' (p. 148). We do not of course speak within inverted commas, but writers use them to enclose dialogue). Queneau was much in sympathy with literary Modernism, with its stress on the creation of autonomous worlds expressed in a new language, and freed from the bondages of conventions such as orthodox concepts of time. He regarded both literature and mathematics less as explanations or even descriptions of everyday reality

[33] See *Saint-Glinglin*, p. 32.
[34] Queneau wrote a study of dog-language in Carroll's *Sylvie and Bruno*.

than as realities to be explored and exalted in their own right: self-sufficient systems, alternative worlds. Is *Zazie dans le métro*, then, an anti-novel filled with anti-heroes? It is and is not. Queneau is at the same time a derivative, assimilating kind of writer (cf. Alain: 'Qui n'imite rien n'invente point'), and a true original, who is starting to be imitated by younger writers in present-day France. A sure sign, in that land of intellectual incest and parasitism, that you have truly arrived, that you are a contemporary classic. Though Queneau repeatedly confessed his debts to Homer, Rabelais, Flaubert, Alfred Jarry, Jacques Prévert, James Joyce and William Faulkner, his own *Le Chiendent* paved the way for Sartre's philosophical novel, *La Nausée*. And Queneau begat Boris Vian, parodist, master of the vernacular, enormously popular with the youth of France for many years now, and a convinced *zazou* himself. In *Zazie dans la métro*, the ancient sceptical tradition is brought up to date, made thoroughly modern. And humour of this variety is proved to be widespread (if not universal) and durable (if not eternal). Just as Balzac had reappearing characters in his *Comédie humaine*, so Queneau has recurring (rhyming) situations, personages, phrases. His fictional world is homogeneous, but not homogenised, so that he does not really need Balzac's device in order to hold the separate bits together. That job is done by a controlling intelligence, sympathy and comic sense.

I suggested earlier that Queneau's style is catching, and so, rather than trying to con-clude about him, I wish to finish with a lyrical pastiche from Brée and Guiton, who say that there is in Queneau's work 'the occasional throbbing note of sadness; the pangs of un-requited love, the remorseless passage of time . . . the inexplicable existence of fleas' (*19*, pp. 173-4). There I must leave you, to scratch yourselves. 'Vous pouvez vous gratter': that is your lot, you will have to provide the rest yourselves.

Bibliography

Dates in brackets refer to first publication.

Place of publication is Paris, and the publisher Gallimard, unless otherwise stated.

WORKS BY QUENEAU

Le Chiendent, 1933.

Les Derniers Jours, 1963 (1936).

Odile, 1937.

Les Enfants du limon, 1938.

Un Rude Hiver, 1939.

Pierrot mon ami, 1942.

Loin de Rueil, 1945.

Exercices de style, 1973 (1947).

Saint-Glinglin, 1948.

Bâtons, chiffres et lettres, 1965 (1950).

Le Dimanche de la vie, 1952.

Zazie dans le métro, 1959.

Cent mille milliards de poèmes, 1961.

Oeuvres complètes de Sally Mara, 1962.

Bords, Hermann, 1963.

Les Fleurs bleues, 1965.

L'Instant fatal, 1966 (1943, 1948).

Le Vol d'Icare, 1968.

Chêne et chien, and *Petite cosmogonie portative*, 1969 (1937, 1950).

Le Voyage en Grèce, 1973.

La Littérature potentielle, a collective work of *Oulipo*, 1973.

BOOKS AND PERIODICALS DEVOTED TO QUENEAU

1. *L'Arc*, 28, 1966.

2. Baligand, Renée, *Les Poèmes de Raymond Queneau*, Ottawa: Didier, 1972.

3. Bens, Jacques, *Queneau*, 1962.

4. Bergens, Andrée, *Raymond Queneau*, Geneva: Droz, 1963.

5. Bergens, Andrée (editor), "Queneau", *Cahiers de l'Herne*, 1975.

6. Daubercies, Claude, *Le Jeu de mots chez Raymond Queneau*, Diplôme d'Etudes Supérieures, Lille University, 1960.

7. *Dossiers du Collège de 'Pataphysique*, 20, July 1962.

8. Duprez, Leif, *Clef pour Zazie dans le métro*, Stockholm: Almqvist and Wiksell, 1972.

9. Gayot, Paul, *Queneau*, Editions Universitaires, 1967.

10. Guicharnaud, Jacques, *Raymond Queneau*, New York, Columbia U.P., 1965.

11. *Magazine littéraire*, 94, 1974.

12. Quéval, Jean, *Raymond Queneau*, Seghers, 1971 (1960).

13. Simonnet, Claude, *Queneau déchiffré*, Julliard, 1962.

14. *Temps Mêlés*, 50-52, 1961.

ARTICLES AND CHAPTERS ON QUENEAU

15. Barthes, Roland, 'Zazie et la littérature', *Critique*, 147/148 (1959), 675-81.

16. Belaval, Yvon, 'Queneau l'Oulimpien', *Critique*, 319 (1973), 1061-74.

17. Borie, Jean, 'Raymond Queneau: poésie et français parlé', *Romanic Review*, 57 (1966), 41-55.

18. Boyer, Régis, 'Mots et jeux de mots chez Prévert, Queneau, Vian, Ionesco,' *Studia Neophilologica*, XL (1968), 317-58.

19. Brée, G. and Guiton, M., *An Age of Fiction*, New Brunswick,

N.J., Rutgers U.P., 1957, 169-79.

20. Camus, Albert, *'Pierrot mon ami'*, in *Essais*, 1965, 1928-30.

21. Doppagne, Albert, 'Le Néologisme chez Raymond Queneau', *CAIEF*, 25 (1973), 91-107.

22. Duras, Marguerite, 'Uneuravek', *L'Express*, 22 January 1959, 27-28.

23. Esslin, Martin, 'Raymond Queneau', in *The Novelist as Philosopher*, ed. John Cruickshank, London: Oxford U.P., 1962, 79-101.

24. Kojève, Alexandre, 'Les Romans de la sagesse', *Critique*, 60 (1952), 387-97.

25. Léon, P., 'Phonétisme, graphisme et zazisme', *Etudes de Linguistique Appliquée*, 1 (1962), 70-84.

26. Mayne, Richard, 'The Queneau Country', *Encounter*, 6 (1965), 64-71.

27. Prince, Gerald, 'Queneau et l'antiroman', *Neophilologus*, 55 (1971), 33-40.

28. Rostand, Jean, 'Queneau et la cosmogonie', *Critique*, 49 (1951), 483-91.

29. Roy, Claude, 'Raymond Queneau', *Poésie 46*, 33 (1946), 79-84.

30. Targe, A., 'Un Métro nommé Bonheur', *Poétique*, 29 (1977), 61-76.

Anyone keen to improve their command of colloquial French should read the excellent *Méthode à Mimile* by Alphonse Boudard and Luc Etienne, Livre de Poche, 1977.